D1334673

The Power of Knowledge in Real Estate & Investments

The Power of Knowledge in Real Estate & Investments

Francesco M. Di Meglio CRES
with illustrations by Sarah Roszler

Writers Club Press
San Jose   New York   Lincoln   Shanghai

The Power of Knowledge in Real Estate & Investments

All Rights Reserved © 2002 by Francesco M. Di Meglio

No part of this book may be reproduced or transmitted in any form or by any means, graphic, electronic, or mechanical, including photocopying, recording, taping, or by any information storage retrieval system, without the permission in writing from the publisher.

Writers Club Press
an imprint of iUniverse, Inc.

For information address:
iUniverse, Inc.
5220 S. 16th St., Suite 200
Lincoln, NE 68512
www.iuniverse.com

ISBN: 0-595-21212-3

Printed in the United States of America

To Contact Author:
Frank Di Meglio
P.O. Box 32
Beaconsfield, Quebec, Canada
H9W 5T6
Email: montebello-fdm@sympatico.ca

CONTENTS

Illustrations: Sarah Roszler

Canadian Cataloguing in Publication Data

Di Meglio, Francesco (Frank)
The power of knowledge in real estate & investments.

Library of Congress Cataloguing in Publication Data

CHAPTER 1

Buying a Home for You and Your Family

After making sacrifices, you have managed to save enough money to make a down payment on your very own personal residence. This in itself is a great achievement. Whether you are a repeat or a first-time buyer, this chapter will help you to consider and evaluate the relevant facts before making your decision to buy a home.

When making the choice of where you are going to purchase your home, you should also take into consideration that one day you may want to sell this property. Both the location and the type of home you buy should have desirable qualities. The greater the demand, the easier it will be to sell. Being near schools, recreational facilities, libraries, shopping areas, hospitals or medical clinics, places of worship, and having good access to the workplace are just some of the things people consider when choosing the general area in which they are going to live. Having friends or family members who also live in the area would be another good reason to locate in a neighborhood.

There is an old saying: "It's easier to upgrade one house on a good street than it is to upgrade the whole street around one house." Selecting the right street is not difficult: a short walk up and down the road will tell you a lot about the people that live there. Well-maintained homes as well as the surrounding landscape indicate the general standards of that street and the neighboring community. It would be wiser to pay more for a home on a well-maintained street than to pay less for the same type of home on a less desirable one. Smaller homes in a mix of much larger homes tend to bring higher prices than those in another area with smaller homes. Conversely, larger homes in an area of predominantly smaller sized homes tend to fetch lower prices than they might in an area of similarly larger homes.

Knowing who your immediate neighbors are is highly recommended before you make a decision to buy a home you like. You are going to be seeing a lot of these people, and it would be nice to know that you will have accommodating neighbors who enjoy exchanging the pleasantries of daily life. Whether you are moving across town or out of town, your new home is going to take some getting used to. If you take the time to select the neighborhood that suits your particular lifestyle and tastes, it is likely that your new neighbors and new community attributes will help make your transition a lot easier.

When you've selected the home you wish to buy, try to spend some time alone in the house. Make several visits. Make sure you see it both during the day and in the evening, if possible. Each visit will give you an added perspective and a different impression. When it feels right, then you know that you are making the right choice.

Suburban or City Living

It's often difficult to choose between the city and the suburbs. It's not as easy to choose as people make it out to be. The suburbs often have larger homes at lower prices, relatively speaking, and usually larger lots, and the suburban lifestyle is totally different from the urban lifestyle.

Let's consider this: Suppose you live in a suburb which is located some 20 to 30 miles from the center of town. Imagine what the plot of land your home is situated on looked like some 50 or 100 years ago. Chances are it was a farm or a forest area, or maybe a country place for city dwellers. What has taken place in most major cities is that as the population gets larger, more and more land around the city center gets eaten up by development of subdivisions for new houses.

As this happens, new sub-cores are created which, in fact, duplicate essentially the exact same things the city core has to offer. These areas become known as satellite centers.

They are usually well planned and offer a range of affordable options for new and first-time home buyers. These new modern homes offer quality living space in terms of size, design and comfort, as well as latest technologies in innovative insulation of walls, windows and roof. Chapter 3 outlines what to look for in a home before you buy.

Then there is the lot surrounding the home. In the suburbs, it is usually much larger than in the downtown area, giving way to convenient playgrounds for the entire family, as well as lush manicured landscapes which are aesthetically pleasing and a joy to maintain for those who have or are developing a green thumb.

What I consider of primary importance in the decision to purchase a home is affordability. The second factor is obviously quality of life, and the third is the costs involved in owning a home. These play a significant role in determining where you are going to live.

If money is no object, obviously your choice is based on quality of life. People in this category are often drawn to areas where the benchmark is $250,000 or more for the least expensive home in that particular area. If you are going to purchase a home in this price range, consider this: How much home are you getting for your money in the city and compare that to the suburbs. More often than not, you are going to get a lot more home for your money in a suburban area than you would in the city. So the next area to consider becomes the quality of life you want to live.

Accessibility

In the city most places are accessible by public transportation, and a family may be able to get by with just one car. In the suburbs, however, a family will probably need two vehicles. Very often, city dwellers have diffi-culty finding space to park their vehicles, whereas in the suburbs this is not a problem. The biggest difference between the city and the suburbs is that everything in the city is more compact: homes are built closer together (sometimes too close for comfort). Almost everything is multi-story. On the other hand, you can walk to most places: the library, local corner gro-cery store, pharmacy, hardware and public indoor and outdoor play-grounds. And, when you don't feel like walking, public transportation is very accessible and affordable, especially when you consider the cost and maintenance of a second car.

In the suburbs, however, everything is spread out. The closest thing you can walk to is your immediate neighbor and in some cases even that requires a second thought. The homes are bigger, the parks are huge, sometimes contiguous, connected for many different types of activities. The shopping areas are often sprawling malls covering acres and acres of commercial activity. I sometimes think that whenever you go to one of these places and park your car, you need a bus to take you to the front door of the shopping center, and then take another bus to take you to your destination.[1]

Cost

A word to the wise. If there is one objective the home buyer should strive for, it is to pay off the house loan or mortgage as soon as possible. Look at a mortgage with payments to amortize the loan over a period of not more than 20 years; you'll come out a winner every time.

---

[1] A note to merchants or to anyone considering in investing in a shopping centre: employees should park their cars in a designated area of the parking lot, so the customers can park closer to the stores. I realize that often the last people to leave the mall are its employees, and having to walk that distance alone can be frightening. The parking lot, however, should be well lit, so this should not be a concern. And consider this: if the mall managers designate an employee parking area, then all employees will be headed towards that one area and in numbers there is security.

Another area of concern is taxes. This one requires a lot of thought because, as you know, taxes almost always go up. Therefore, the amount of taxes you start with when you buy a property will very often escalate with time until you decide to sell. Most often the taxes in an area located close to downtown are very high, often higher than in the suburbs.

Mind you, not all suburbs are alike and therefore they have different tax systems and tax bases. Although the taxes are higher near the core, the rate of increase is very often lower, due to the fact that the infrastructure (roads, sidewalks, water and sewage systems) is already in place, having been paid for over the years, and the only cost to the tax payers is upkeep and maintenance of the infrastructure.

In the suburbs, as newer communities, these same infrastructure costs are still being paid for. And, as newer subdivisions are added on to existing ones, these costs are spread over the entire community. This brings up the cost of taxes for everyone.

There are some things you should consider which may determine the cost-efficiency of the community in which you decide to live. A well-organized community very often has a good commercial and industrial base which shoulders most of the tax increases. Therefore, when taxes do go up, the industrial and commercial sectors will pay the brunt of the load and the amount of taxes the home owners will have to pay will be less.

Another point you should consider is that if the suburban town in which you decide to buy a home has paid for the partial or total cost of the infrastructure, you may be able to buy down the costs that affect your home and thereby lower your taxes forever. Wouldn't that be wonderful. Hard to believe? Allow me to explain how it works and you will see how this is not only possible but could make your entire community a better place to live, not only for you but for everyone. Who knows, they may even ask you to help run the place!

When the powers-that-be are going to develop a new subdivision, they must decide who is going to pay for the costs. A tract of land that is to be properly subdivided must have parks for green space; therefore a percentage of the total area under development is designated as green space. This could be 5 to 10% of the total land area being subdivided. Another percentage of the total area is designated for roads and sidewalks which will house the water, sewer and electrical systems which will provide the community services as we call them. The costs of installing this infrastructure is very high and is sometimes shared by the town and the developer.

In cases where the town has picked up part of, or in some cases, the total cost of the infrastructure, the council will have to pass a by-law to borrow the money and pay back the cost of borrowing. When this happens, most towns borrow money and pay it over a period of 25 years. The amortization of this loan is negotiated so that every 5 years the rate would be adjusted to reflect current market interest rates. This means that you can ask the municipal tax authorities to allow you to pay part of or the total outstanding amount borrowed that affects your lot. This can be done whenever a loan becomes due.

By the way, whenever your town goes to borrow money for whatever reason, if they can't amortize the loan over 10 to 15 years, they should not borrow the money at all. The reason is simple: the lower the amortization period, the less interest you pay because you are paying off the loan in less time. Of course the best way would be to pay for the cost of the infrastructure in cash. However, this is not always possible and requires leaders who have both foresight and a highly developed sense of community responsibility not to tax their ratepayers' future to the hilt.

This brings us to another point. If the town didn't pay for the services, then the developer of the land did, and incorporated the cost of these services into the selling price of the house. Once the house is paid for, the cost of the services has been paid forever.

Another check and balance before you buy that dream home is to go to city hall and talk to the tax department. Ask what the taxes have been for the last five years (the tax history) and see what increase, if any, has taken place over that period of time. This will give you a better idea of what may take place over the next five years.

A word to the buyers of new houses: before you sign on the dotted line, find out who paid for the infrastructure in the development: the municipality or town or the developer. Then ask the magic question: how much are the taxes going to be, since this is a new property and has no historical tax record. And, yes, get it in writing. Don't accept a verbal statement of the amount; get them to commit in writing to an amount with a range of not more than $300 either way. They will often tell you they cannot give you an exact amount because they don't know the final evaluation of the house; this is true, but evaluations are based on square footage of the property and therefore they know the rate of taxes (mill rate) to charge for every $100 of evaluation. This way they can give you an approximate amount of what you'll end up paying.

By the way, there is a little known secret you should know about. The town authority and the developer may have a private agreement and it goes like this. The developer is not assessed any taxes on the construction of the new home until the property is sold to a home buyer. This allows a developer a lot of leeway. However, he must pay the taxes on the land during the interim between the time the house is built until it is finally sold. The reason for this is that a house that has been built by a developer is not considered finished until it is occupied and someone is living there. That makes perfect sense. However, if the construction is not completed, a proper evaluation cannot take place until it is finished.

> This reminds me of a story a padre friend of mine told me. He claims that someone he knew on a South Seas Island had submitted a plan for his home to the town authorities 65 years ago but never completed the entire plan. He is living in a virtually completed home, and, yes, you guessed it, he hasn't paid a cent in taxes since that time, the crafty old fellow. How much money did he save over the years? I hope they don't nail him for back taxes…

While we're on the subject there's something I've been wanting to say about the way property taxes are assessed. This may or may not be the tax system that's in place in your community. If it is, it's time to change it. Taxes are assessed based on a formula, the rate being so much per $100.00 of evaluation. This amount is called the mill rate. I'll give you an example: let's say the mill rate is $1.21 per 100.00 dollar evaluation and let's say the value of your home is $100,000. That means that the taxes you'd pay per year would be $1,210. That seems to be easy enough.

Where the problem arises is when someone decides to improve his home. Suppose the homeowner finishes the basement, adds new windows and new doors, and in so doing, improves the value of his or her home by, let's say, 10 to 15%. The town comes along and inspects the property, which they have a right to do once every two or three years. The evaluators will deem the value of the property to have gone up, so the taxes go up, pro-rated to the new evaluation.

Let's think this through, folks; this is the most senseless form of taxation I've ever heard of. A home owner has gone out of his or her way to improve the quality of lifestyle in his or her home; purchased new materials; created employment; improved or maintained the quality of the neighborhood—and the town asks the homeowner to pay more taxes for doing so. Well, if that's the case, should they lower the taxes for people who don't do any improvements to their property?

Can you make sense of this? The system punishes an individual for improving his property! This is totally wrong and should be changed to a fairer system. I agree that if you add an extension to your home, you should pay more because you've increased the size of the house. But it doesn't seem fair that by making a house more comfortable and useful (such as by finishing the basement) or by carrying out needed repairs such as re-roofing, re-siding or putting in new windows (thereby creating employment), the homeowner should be socked with a higher evaluation, and higher property taxes.

Or, how about this one? The value of a home goes up, therefore the taxes go up. Why? Why should you pay more just because the house has gone up in value. If no one sold their home, there would be no new value, right, so the system punishes people who don't sell their home. I'm thinking of older folks who love their home, who are on a pension or a fixed income and are forced to sell their property because they can't afford the taxes...Does that make sense to you? Well, this is happening everywhere, and it's time to stop this practice and change the way the tax system works because this is wrong. To those towns that have made changes to reflect these concerns, I take my hat off, and wish there are more of them around. I hope this book gets people moving in towns where the tax system penalizes people who maintain and improve their homes.

CHAPTER 2

Your Home and
How It's Made, or Should Be...

Most homes are built today to conform to the standards of the National Building Code. These standards are constantly being upgraded to reflect new technologies in material and workmanship. Before a home can be constructed, a building permit must be issued by the county or municipality. Before a permit is issued, a plan must be submitted, showing the layout and identifying materials to be used to complete the project. The municipal building inspector will check that the proposed project is in conformity with the building code before issuing a permit. The home owner may take comfort knowing that the home is built to norms, and is therefore safe, and that the materials used meet the standard of the building industry.

However, some builders cut corners to save a few dollars. I would like to illustrate the different options available to you, the consumer. The Code outlines the very basic method of building and it's up to you if you want to exceed those standards or not. Just make sure you are not compromised by poor quality workmanship or sloppy workers. If you use the best quality material money can buy and hire a contractor who doesn't pay attention to detail in both implementation and installation of material and workmanship, you have thrown good money away. I've seen million-dollar homes as well as $70,000 homes being built by sloppy contractors who don't take pride in their work. The result is always the same. The contractor blames the sub-trades, the sub-trades blame each other, and you, the consumer, are left holding the short end of the stick. What it all boils down to is you have to insist on quality of installation and workmanship, and anything less is not acceptable. I believe there are two ways of doing things; the right way and my way and they are both one and the same.

Now let's look at what components should be used in today's home industry. If you are buying a new home or having one built, you will be able to benefit from this knowledge. I will take you through the process of building a home and then talk about older homes and how they too can be brought up to today's standards.

New Construction

Foundations

The foundation and footings of a home haven't changed that much over the years. However, today we are using better quality cement along with a key or lock to connect the footings with the foundation walls. What this means is that when the footings are installed at the base which becomes the support for the foundation walls, a groove or key is made along the center of the footings, usually the size of a 2 x 4.

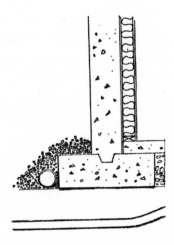

This cavity is created to allow the concrete wall to be erected along the center of this groove; it enables the wall to lock in place and more or less become one with the footings and foundation walls. This method prevents any water from coming inside the walls.

Foundation Drainage and Plumbing Notes

Once the foundation has been poured, black pitch is sprayed on the outside walls of the footings. This acts as a water sealer to prevent moisture or water from penetrating the walls. We've perfected the tile drain system which rests on the footing along the outside of the foundation walls and connects to a sump pump on the inside of the building. This allows any excess water which accumulates outside along the foundation walls and does not drain away into the earth to be fed into a pit by way of the tile drain. The pump is placed in this pit, then water is pumped into the drain system of the house or pumped outside away from the house to avoid causing damage to the foundation. What makes our modern tile drain system even better is that there is almost no chance for the pipe to be blocked. This is due to the fact that the pipe used for drainage has a veil surrounding it, which allows water to enter the system, and prevents sand

and earth from accumulating inside. When the system is installed properly, with gravel covering the pipe before the earth is backfilled, you're almost guaranteed a trouble-free system, and you will not have to worry about water entering your home.

When pouring the basement floor, make sure proper sloping drains are installed in the floor in case you want to wash it down or in case a pipe breaks. The water can be drained without too much effort and without causing much damage. Before pouring the 6" concrete floor, install a 6-10 ml. polyethylene film on top of the vapor barrier. This reduces humidity penetration. Then add a wire mesh on top of the vapor barrier; this unifies the concrete floor and prevents it from cracking. Be sure to install a backwater valve in your sewer system. This mechanical device is a flap that rests inside a pipe. It allows water and sewer drainage to leave your home, and blocks any sewer backup from coming back into your system. When water pressure occurs on one side, the valve opens and allows water to leave your home.

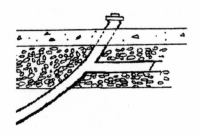

When pressure comes from the outside the home, the flap closes shut and prevents sewage from re-entering the plumbing system in your home. This little gadget has saved millions of dollars in property damage, and offers a lot of peace of mind. In fact, the insurance company may not pay for damage caused by water backing up if you don't have this valve installed. (I will talk more about insurance companies in a later chapter.)

Have you ever taken a shower, and, right in the middle of it, someone in the house decides to flush the toilet? All of a sudden that nice hot shower becomes even hotter, so much hotter that you are almost scalded. You think to yourself, "I wish that person who just flushed the toilet had been more considerate. He could have waited until my shower was over!" You make a quick adjustment of the water mix only to discover that the water pressure has gone down; now you seem to be getting only hot water and no cold water to give you your selected temperature mix. If this has ever happened to you, there is a way to correct this problem once and for all. Instead of installing a 1/2" line throughout the whole house, install a 3/4" line to feed all your water outlets for both hot and cold water lines. By the way, this will also eliminate that annoying noise in the water line you hear when someone is taking a shower. Sure, 3/4" inch line will cost a little more, but think of the pleasure and benefit you will get from this little added feature to your home. Now you can take a shower with little risk of sudden changes in water temperature.

By the way, if you can't change all the pipes in your home to get this convenience, there is a new water faucet on the market that you can install. This faucet will maintain a constant water temperature during the time of your shower; however, it's not cheap and will have to be replaced with time, but it is a less expensive alternative for those of you that cannot change the water lines in your home.

Framing and Insulation

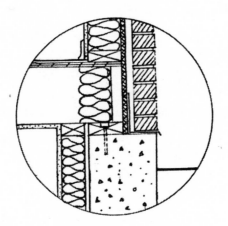

Our next concern is the framing of the exterior walls. There are many ways to achieve the same result and for good reason. We are fortunate to have such a variety of options to fit different budgets. For those of you who don't know what framing means, I will explain. When building a home, you must put up an outside wall to hold up the house. Framing refers to the material used to hold this wall in place. Many different types of material are used to suit different needs and climates. For example, if you are living in a climate that has very cold winters, you would use materials that would allow you to add enough insulation for comfort. Studs, 2"x 4"x 8' uprights, are commonly used to frame a home as well as to erect dividing walls. The 2"x 4" method is used in less expensive homes, what are called "starter homes" or what the industry refers to as homes for first-time buyers. This method allows for 4" of insulation to be placed between the studs, and requires an outside fibreboard sheathing membrane which forms a weather barrier and adds rigidity to the frame. The exterior wall may then be finished in brick, clapboard or aluminum or vinyl siding, all of which achieve different, aesthetically pleasing finishes. Or, in some cases, a combination of two or more types of materials is used to give the home balance. Obviously if you use only aluminum or clapboard, it would be less expensive than if you were to use all brick or all stone.

Very often, builders use a combination of materials to add character to a home. In all cases, an overlapped plastic vapor barrier must be installed on the inside of the outside walls of your home. This cuts down the amount of heat lost in the cold winter months. Then you would install a gypsum board finish over the plastic vapor barrier to complete the inside finish.

As I said this is a very basic method and one which should not be compromised. In more expensive homes, a 2"x 6"x 8' stud is used to frame a home. This allows the builder to use 6" of insulation instead of 4" and therefore gives you a higher insulating factor or R-value. Using this method, a wider foundation wall must be installed to allow for the space required to receive the additional 2" of wood..In areas where the climate is warmer and winters are not severe, cinder blocks are used to erect outside walls and are finished in stucco on the outside to complete the exterior finish. This method is very cost-efficient, and very often different methods of applying stucco are used to complete the look of the home.

My purpose is not to illustrate all the different types of walls one can use to build a home, but rather to point out the very basic standard one should consider when building a home in most parts of North America.

The Roof, Insulation and Ventilation

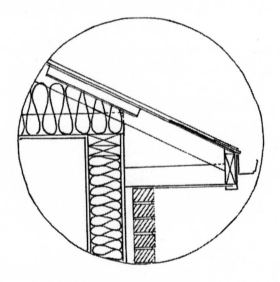

Adding extra insulation in the attic allows you to keep your cost of heating and air conditioning down. The norm is an insulation factor of R-32. You can bring this up to R-40 which will achieve better results. This may be added in the attic between the joists or on top of the joints. When completing the roof, a 5/8" tongue and groove plywood is the ideal product to complete the underlay or membrane part of the roof. I like to believe that you could have a party up there and not fall through.

Careful consideration must be given to what type of roof is needed. If you have a flat roof, then obviously a stronger wood like a 3/4" plywood would be used, whereas in a slopping roof 3/4" is really not necessary. However, the choice is yours. The roof is one of the key functions of your home; if you want a stronger roof, insist on upgrading the type of wood used. Once you've completed your home, you shouldn't have to say, "Gee, I wish I had put a 3/4" plywood instead of 3/8"!" It's too late then.

On a flat roof, you want to make sure that there is a nice, gentle slope in the roof design leading to a drain or several drains, as the case may be. Each drain must have a basket strainer that allows water to run freely into the drain but keeps leaves and other debris out. If the drains are blocked, the water can back up when it rains and come into the house between the outside walls and cause a lot of damage. Check roof drains regularly to make sure they are clear and not blocked with leaves, as often happens.

On a sloping roof, careful consideration must be given to completing the finishing. I recommend that black paper be installed on the entire roof as well as a 3'-6' wide rolled tar (called an ice and water shield) on the perimeter of the roof. This prevents any ice forming and backing up under shingles. I would insist on the ice and water shield installation, otherwise you will have to install an electrical wire on top of your shingles to prevent any ice build-up in colder climates. In this case, an ounce of prevention is worth a pound of cure.

Now we come to the shingles themselves. Most shingles have a life expectancy of 10 to 40 years. The type you should use depends on your budget. Obviously the longer the life span of the shingle, the more it's going to cost. But, since the cost of installing the shingles is the same, why do it twice in 20 years?

The ventilation of your roof is very important and if it is not done right can lead to problems that will cause your roof to rot without your knowledge. There are many types of roof vents and all perform well. However, some are better than others in different circumstances. I would say that most mechanical vents would have to be replaced more often than the conventional ones. In all cases, one vent should be installed for every 350 sq. ft. of your roof. Don't compromise here.

Heating and Air Conditioning

When choosing a heating system for your home, serious consideration must be given to the type of climate you live in. One of the most talked about heating and air-conditioning systems is a heat pump, and rightly so because it serves a dual purpose. Some people love heat pumps and some people hate them and both have good reasons. Here is why. You first must understand how the system works. A heat pump is based on the same principal as a refrigerator. Air is drawn into the system. The air is made of both cold and hot molecules. In the summer months, the system separates the air molecules and discharges the hot and keeps the cold; in the winter, the reverse happens.

Sounds pretty easy, doesn't it, and it is. Except when you install this system on the wrong part of the planet. If you live in Winnipeg, Canada, considered to be one of the coldest places on earth, this system will not give you the heating comfort you need throughout the winter months without a backup oil or gas system to supplement the heat. You see, this system does not work in very severe extreme temperatures without a backup system. However, if you live in a more temperate climate, this same system will deliver comfortable heat with little effort and no backup required. So, I would only recommend installing a heat pump if you live in an area where temperatures are not very cold. If you live in areas where the variation in climate is extreme, I would strongly recommend that you install separate systems, one to heat, and another to air-condition your home.

Another problem is that heat pumps are sometimes installed without careful consideration of how cold and hot air are transferred from one point to another. When installing a heat pump, you must install a duct system for warmed or cooled air to be transferred throughout your home. As you know, hot air rises and cold air falls. Knowing this, when installing a heat pump in a two-story cottage, you must install adequate vents to move both cold and hot air. Since cold air is harder to move upwards than warm, you must increase the size of your ducting system to allow cold air to move freely. Most systems are installed with 3" to 4" extension vents leading to each room in the home and this will work well for heating. However, you will not get the same results when you want to air-condition your home and therefore you must use 5" to 6" extension vents; these will allow cold air to move freely and give you the comfort you want throughout the hot summer months.

As you can see when installing a heat pump in an existing home with 3" to 4" extension vents, the heating part will work well. However, the air conditioning will not be adequate due to the difficulty of moving cold air throughout your home. It is difficult to correct the problem and change the existing ducting system because most of it is behind finished walls and floorboards. However, some corrective measures may be taken to alleviate this problem. Since cold air stays in the basement of your home, you would install one or two air return ducts (depending on the size of your home) leading back to the air-conditioning unit, and thereby allow air to re-circulate throughout your home and provide greater comfort.

I should like to point out that if you intend to heat your home with electric baseboard heaters, the temperature setting should be the same in every room throughout your home; otherwise you will end up paying more to heat less. Electric baseboard heating should only be installed where the outside walls and roof are well insulated to prevent heat loss. In new homes, this means the walls should have an R-20 rating and the roof, an R-40 rating for insulation. The more insulation you have, the higher the rating factor becomes.

A word of advice: if you have an electric heating system, get a humidifier to supplement moisture in your home. Or hang up your laundry inside. As it dries, it will provide adequate moisture and allow you to save on electricity consumption. The electric baseboard system only works well when you have the correct number of heaters needed to produce enough

B.T.U. (British thermal units) to satisfy your temperature requirements. In this case, more is better, for example if your heaters have a capacity to produce more heat than required, this will allow your heaters to work at medium strength rather than maximum capacity when the weather becomes extremely cold. Wall thermostats should always be installed on the inside, not outside, of dividing walls, to give you properly regulated heat. This applies to all forms of heating systems.

A hot water radiator system is considered by many to be one of the best forms of heating in terms of cost efficiency and maximum comfort, but it is very costly to install. Unlike electric radiators, the hot water in the radiators will continue to give off heat long after the furnace has shut down. This form of heating may use one of three types of energy: natural gas, oil or electricity to supply the heat required to warm the water. My preference is oil, because this fuel very often can be supplied by competitive dealers whose prices are not always regulated and who provide very good service. To jump ship from gas to electric or oil can be an expensive trip, unless you have a system on the furnace that allows you to do it; then you're in the driver's seat. Some large users of energy have a feature on their furnaces that gives them this flexibility.

I believe competition brings out the best in people. Unlike the gas or electrical companies whose prices are set…and guess what happens if you don't like their service or price? They are the only show in town—too bad, so sad.

Speaking of cheap energy, I can't wait until someone invents an electrical meter to determine the time of day you use electricity. This way, electrical companies can offer cheaper rates when demand is low. So if you know someone who is either in the process of inventing or has invented one, let's get out there and let these companies know about it, and let's start using meters. Look at it this way: if your electrical company gets the energy from a hydro dam project, the water that turns the turbines that produces electricity is always running, so when the demand is low, some of the turbines are turned off.

These same turbines could be kept on with zero waste of energy. I hope this comes to pass and we can all enjoy the benefits of cheaper electricity.

By the way, our next source of energy is going to be solar and wind energy. To tap into these forms of energy will be our next challenge. The wheels are already in motion and it's just a question of time before a major breakthrough comes about and makes these new energy sources accessible to all.

Summer Cooling

As an alternative or as a complement to air-conditioning, you might consider installing ceiling fans in every room. These fans are inexpensive and can be operated in both summer and winter. In both cases fans keep air moving; in winter they can push down heated air that rises to the ceiling, and in summer they can pull hot air up towards the ceiling and keep cool air down. Most fans have a forward and reverse switch.

Windows

Windows are going to be a major expense. This is one area where you should not compromise: you must pay for quality and durability. Double hung windows are a thing of the past and have been replaced by thermopane windows. These are made of two thick panes of vacuum-sealed glass with a space between the panes to form a kind of vapor barrier. A new twist has been added: a gas called argon can be injected in between the two panes and sealed so that it cannot escape. This prevents heat from escaping or entering as the case may be for winter or summer. It is not a "must-have" feature but one worth considering when installing new windows.

In selecting the best kind of windows for your home, careful consideration must be given to the climate and variable temperature where you live. If you live in an area where temperatures reach extremes, by this I mean very hot and very cold, you should use thermopane windows. This will allow you to maintain comfort levels throughout the year more economically. Otherwise simple double pane, double diamond windows are sufficient and more economical to install.

If you have a choice as to what type of window opening to get, you should get sash windows, the ones that go up and down, rather than the crank ones that open to the outside. The up and down kind will give you flexibility when it's raining, and allow air to circulate freely from top and bottom openings, whereas this may be more difficult with an entire window that opens to the outside. You will probably want to close crank windows when it rains, since both air and water can come in through the entire opening, whereas the sash type can be regulated to give you maximum comfort.

Imagine leaving your house with some windows open, and while you're away a storm comes up... Which kind of window would you prefer to have left open? Chances are you would choose sash windows; air can come in and go out freely, without creating gusts of wind which will make your curtains fly all over the place and allow both wind and water to come in.

Sliding windows behave much the same way as the crank type that opens to the outside. Once the window is open, air comes in through the entire opening. However, sliding windows usually have two sets of panes that open from left to right and right to left, an inner and outer set. With this type you can best regulate air flow by opening the outside left or right pane and keeping the opposite inside pane open. This feature will not only allow air to circulate freely but will do so safely, preventing free access to anyone wishing to enter.

Aesthetics play an important role in choosing the right kind of window and rightly so. Windows often dress up a home, and the size and kind you choose should enhance the overall design and provide the kind of comfort you desire.

Electricity and Power

As you know, the electronic age is upon us, and with this comes the need for more electricity. Having the right size of electrical entrance can often save you money. By this I mean that if you don't have enough electrical power, you may have to install a new panel, incurring a costly visit from an electrician when you realize your electrical needs are more than what your panel and entry can supply. My suggestion is to discuss your electrical energy needs with an electrician. He will advise you on the type of installation you require, taking into consideration the type of heating system you plan to use in your home, whether you want to install an air conditioner or not, not to mention dryers, dishwashers and so on that are used on a daily basis.

Most homes have a 200-amp entrance which satisfies most requirements. The cost saving of installing a 100-amp versus a 200-amp is minimal, so why not install a 200-amp; the cost saving is not worth the hassle.

Features to Consider When Building Your Home

Kitchens

Everyone loves a large kitchen, but both designers and architects and builders don't seem to know that, and still build homes with small kitchens. Designers **will** design the perfect kitchen for a three-bedroom home into a 5-bedroom home. I can't figure out why. This is the place where the family spends most of their time, so why not build a large enough room to accommodate everyone and family activities.

Designing today's kitchen has to be, without a doubt, an enormous challenge. With all the new and modern features and components available, one would have to say that the only limitation is your budget or bank book. Here is my list of features that I think would not only enhance everyone's favorite place to be but also make working or being in the kitchen more enjoyable.

For starters, when planning your kitchen space, try to determine a location where more than one person can put together a meal without getting in each other's way. Sometimes an island makes a great place to carry out multiple functions. Next I would evaluate the amount of counter space needed. And, by the way, try to round off the edges; many hips will thank you.

Once the counter area has been determined, design the cupboard and drawer space in a functional manner. Consider carefully the placement of built-in features such as dishwasher, oven, microwave and refrigerator. If possible, make room for a good-sized pantry. Sometimes counter space can also be used as a breakfast area with bar stools as chairs. Try to maximize the amount of natural light coming into the working area with large windows. Adding false beams to the ceiling can enhance the look, and is also a convenient way of getting additional space to hang pans, fruit baskets, and even dry bunches of herbs.

Washer and Dryer

Washer and dryer facilities should be installed as close to the kitchen as possible. A room of its own would be ideal when you consider that clothes have to be separated for different wash loads, dried and ironed. Often you can't do all of these at once, so it would be nice to just close off this room and walk away.

Closets

Large closet space is another desirable feature and one worth considering. You can never have enough closet space. One area should be a double-rung closet. When visitors are coming, your clothes could be placed at the back and visitors could use the front; this way you don't have to move clothes all over the house and back again. Also consider installing a light in these cupboards, a feature often overlooked.

CHAPTER 3

"Repair and Renovation"

If you can afford it, it's always better to over-build the size of your home rather than make it a perfect fit. Renovating your home can be a joy or a nightmare. A proper planned strategy and careful planning can make the difference. Always try to do repairs in the order of priority and what makes the most sense. For example, don't carry out costly interior renovation without first repairing your roof. Repair leaky exterior foundation walls prior to finishing the basement or upgrading the landscape outside your home. Always carry out repairs in a descending order: upper floors first, than lower floors and so on.

Renovating an Older Home

Always make sure you have installed the right amount of insulation in accordance with the type of heating system you have. When working on an older home, this can be especially important.

Kitchen and Bathroom Upgrade

When upgrading a kitchen or a bathroom in a home older than 25 years old, my suggestion is to start from scratch. By this I mean if you're going to change the cupboards and counters, consider whether you have enough counter plugs or lighting and microwave or counter outlets, and whether you have the proper wiring to make your kitchen functional. A microwave oven requires a designated plug. This means that you have to run a separate wire from the panel to the plug, otherwise, it may cause your circuit breaker or fuse box to trip.

Since you may have to open up some walls, why not change all the old pipes to copper and while you're at it why not re-insulate the inside of the outside walls. Since you need to hire a electrician, why not change that old fuse box panel to a new breaker type. You may want to change that small narrow window and make it bigger and now would be a perfect time to do it. When ordering new counters and cupboards for your kitchen, always make a layout on paper and carefully study it for a few days before ordering it. Try to imagine how functional it would be.

Some older homes can be modified in various ways to meet today's needs. Sometimes removing or shifting a wall, or making an opening in it can make all the difference in allowing you to make use of the space.

When replacing the tiles in the bathroom, change all the old water pipes and drains and install proper electrical outlets to meet today's standards.

When repairing plaster walls that have many cracks in them, it may be far easier to install new gypsum board on top of the old walls. You will get a better result and it will cost less than repairing the walls.

Selecting a Contractor

When contracting out your renovation needs, consider the following very carefully. Call several contractors and get references related to previous jobs they have undertaken. Go and see them if you can, and talk to people who hired them. Ask questions, lots of questions; you know the kind I mean. Ask, "Were you satisfied with the job? Did he do the job on schedule?" (This is very important because sometimes contractors drag out work for weeks on end or use the excuse that a required part is on back order. Whatever the excuse, most can be avoided if the job is planned properly.)

If you are doing work in the kitchen or bathroom, you want the contractor and workers out of there as soon as possible. Contractors seem to forget you live there and have to use these facilities. Before contracting out the work, be sure the work to be carried out and the material to be used is properly specified, the method of payment agreed upon, and the cost defined, the schedule for completion of the work is clear; and, yes, state a penalty if the contractor exceeds that time. When the work is completed, ask the contractor for a list of sub-trades that worked on the project. Make sure all the subcontractors have been paid before making your final payment to the contractor you hired to carry out all the work.

When you write up the contract for the work and cost of the project, I suggest that you state in the contract that you will hold back 20% of the total cost until the contractor has supplied you with a waiver stating that the sub-contractors have been paid in full. If the contractor is going to do all the work himself (with his own workers), you will hold back 10% of the cost and make that final payment 30 days after all the work has been completed to your complete satisfaction as stated on your contract. Good luck and enjoy your renovation project. Remember it's all in the planning!

CHAPTER 4

Buying or Selling Your Home

How To Choose a Good Realtor

Most successful people tend to have unique talents and special qualities. In the real estate business, for example, 20% of all realtors do 80% of the business. That is an incredible statistic-but true! Some people work as realtors on a part-time basis and attempt to carry out their responsibilities to their clients with a minimum of effort. Some of them capitalize on being part of a large firm with credentials. Maybe that's why some of them belong to the 80% side of things!

When you are choosing a realtor, remember what I said about the 20% that do 80% of the work, and make your choice based on individual merit and not necessarily on the size of the agent's company. If you are going to sell your property or buy one, the agent you're dealing with should have access to or be a member of a board of realtors with a web site that makes information about all properties available for sale to potential buyers and all realtors as a matter of course.

The rules of doing business in the real estate world have changed. Although these new rules apply to everyone who has a license to sell real estate, it will not affect the 20% who are successful in the way they conduct themselves in doing business. The big change is that a realtor must now indicate and state clearly his or her position and who he or she represents: the vendor or the purchaser in a transaction. This way the agent's ethics are not compromised because his or her responsibility lies with one person only, not with both buyer and seller. It was evident that agents should not be asked to serve two masters although most good agents, if not all, filled that role of dual representation admirably. After all, if you think about it, both buyer and seller have to be in total agreement before a transaction can be realized. This dual role, however, is difficult unless one is completely open in revealing all the facts honestly to both seller and buyer at all times.

This brings me to the qualities that a good agent must have to achieve success in the profession. A good agent must prioritize his or her role in the profession, and money cannot be at the top of the list. Although it's very close to the top, it is not the Number One priority. The agent must place clear emphasis on the client's needs, have a good market knowledge and good instincts, and answer questions clearly, not vaguely. If the client asks a question the realtor can't answer, the realtor should say so, and add that after making inquiries, he or she will get back to the client—and do it. The realtor must be honest at all times. My grandfather used to tell me that lies have short legs. Revealing all of the facts consistently is without question the most important quality an agent must have at all times. If your agent is not honest and sincere, I would suggest you part company with this individual. Very few people want to deal with an agent who has difficulty understanding the responsibility which has been entrusted to him or her.

I was once introduced to a very wealthy investor from Hong Kong. My role was clear from the start; he was seeking good, safe, long term investments, somewhere he could place his capital and get a return on his investment without too much risk. Well, it took six months before he made his first offer with me. The reason was that he wanted to check and verify all of the facts on several locations I had proposed before he could rely on my information. Once it was established that I provided accurate facts about the properties I had proposed, he was also able to trust my judgement call on each of the sites. He went on to purchase millions of dollars worth of real estate from me. This would never have happened if he did not trust me. I never compromised his trust in me, because my priority was to provide this foreign investor with factual information, and to be honest and sincere, guided by his best interests. Without this, I would never have succeeded in selling any real estate at all.

A good realtor must earn his clients' trust from the beginning of the relationship; otherwise he will not be trusted when it comes to making hard decisions about buying or selling. By the way, most clients can see right through subterfuge anyway. A realtor cannot pretend to give some of the facts some of the time; he or she must do it consistently.

When I first started in my real estate career, I was 21 years of age. Most of my clients were of Italian origin, people who came here hoping to find and provide a better way of life for themselves and their families as most did. These people worked very hard to earn the few dollars that they made. They would put away some money each and every week like my parents did, hoping one day to purchase a home of their own. Most of them did not know how to read or write English; some of them did not even know what a cheque was.

I was given a huge responsibility: to find them a home they could buy and in which they could be comfortable, with affordable payments, which would be a good, sound investment; to show all of the pluses and minuses of the property; to negotiate a fair price to pay for the property; to make arrangements to sign the deed of sale with an honest and reliable notary or lawyer who would not gouge them and would still provide quality services; to arrange insurance for their new home; to arrange for a mortgage and get a competitive interest rate; to fill out cheques each month to pay the mortgage as well as the hydro and oil companies which provided electricity and heating. I was entrusted with the savings of their lifetimes. I could have made a fortune of money dishonestly. Instead, I made more honestly and got recommended to all of their friends and families.

While most agents were experiencing difficulty in selling properties, as is often the case in Montreal's volatile political market, I was inundated with work, often closing transactions in the wee hours of the morning. The people I represented then are still sending me clients today, because I never compromised their trust and that's worth more than money in the bank. There's an old saying which is still true today, "Sooner or later people will find you out, so why not do the right thing." I was often told by my father, "Do for others what you would have others do for you," and that's been my motto in life as well as in business. If we all followed this simple rule, we would find ourselves in a much richer society.

A good realtor is worth his weight in gold, many times over. Realtors sell properties day in day out, but clients may buy or sell a home once, twice or three times in a lifetime. It should be a pleasant experience, and choosing the right realtor for your needs can make that happen.

Recently a good friend of mine, a realtor from a well-known company, told me the following story. He listed a property one day. That same day, he brought a client over to the house and sold it; the ink wasn't even dry on the mandate. How's that for service! Some people might think, "Maybe I listed the property too low, that's why it sold so fast!" Others would think the agent earned a lot of money in just a short time; maybe his commission should have been cut—after all, it took less than 24 hours to close the deal. It's all a matter of perspective, of the way you see things.

If you had done your homework when you selected your agent, you would know that the individual you selected to represent you had a good knowledge of what's going on in the real estate market backed up with substantiated facts, which you had seen and felt confident with. After you had seen the sales in your area, you were able to make a well-informed decision about what price the property was worth in today's real estate market. I would have to say that realtor saved you a lot of time and money, and that he was able to satisfy your needs quickly and efficiently. He certainly earned his keep if not a bonus to boot!

Some people think that because they aren't getting their price, they should be patient and wait until they do. If your property is on the market for a long time, what have you accomplished? Every month that goes by, the property is costing you money, so the less time it takes to sell your property, the better. Then you can move on with your life. You don't need the hassles of keeping the property on the market for longer than necessary. What happens if the market starts to drop? Then your price would fall. You don't need that.

Here is a thought to consider: If you sell your property in a low market, then your next purchase will also be in a low market. The same applies in a rising market, so the sooner you do it, the sooner everyone will be able to satisfy his needs.

The secret in selling your home is very simple; make sure your property has been well maintained. If not, do the basics even before you show it to interview agents you are considering hiring. (See list of Suggestions to help you sell your property, p. 35)

Then, select the right agent who will do the job right. He or she should be able to give an outline of what he or she intends to do to sell your property within a given time frame, usually three months. Try to select an agent who has other listings in your immediate area. Some agents specialize and concentrate their efforts in one particular section of a community. They make it a point to know all there is to know that would effect the value of real estate as well as what properties are selling for.

When you have interviewed all of the agents and found out what the market value of your home is, don't necessarily choose the highest price. Try to be within 5 to 10% of the fair market value if possible. Remember: no one knows the absolute value of your property other than someone who is ready to pay for it at that time. It may be slightly less than what you thought it would be, but don't pass up a good sale because you aren't getting that magic price you have in mind. Let the buyer feel he got the property for a good price because you left some money on the table, and walk away. So many greedy people have let sales slip through their fingers because they wanted every last dollar, only to realize that their property is still for sale months later. Sometimes they have to bite the bullet and drop their price because the market value has dropped. When a property is for sale too long on the market, there is something wrong with it, or with the price, or both.

One question most buyers ask is how long has the property been for sale. If the property has been on the market for a long time, buyers tend to shy away from it fearing there is something wrong with it, and if they do decide to make an offer it's often much lower than the asking price.

One last word of advice: if you can, give yourself enough time to sell your property. Do it at a time when you are not forced to do so. Have the foresight to make it happen when the choice is yours to make and try not to have it forced upon you.

Some Suggestions to Help You Sell Your Property

1. The first impression is a lasting one. Keep your lawn trimmed and edged and flower beds cultivated. Driveway and walkway should be maintained free and clear of refuse. In winter remove snow and ice from walkway and garage access area.

2. Redecorate your property. Faded paint and worn woodwork can reduce desire. Use neutral colors to give the rooms a fresh look.

3. Fix that faucet. Dripping water can discolor enamel and will call attention to faulty plumbing. Remove mildew stains and re-grout tiles to give that sparkling clean look.

4. Hire a carpenter for a day. Loose door knobs, sticking drawers, warped doors and the like should be repaired or replaced.

5. Clear up and clean out from top to bottom. Remove all unnecessary articles which have accumulated to avoid that cluttered look. Clothes should be properly hung up, and shoes, hats and other articles should be neatly stored. This will make your closets look spacious and roomy.

6. In the kitchen, colorful curtains in harmony with the floor and counter-tops add appeal.

7. Light up your house. Make sure all lights are functional. At night, turn on the outside lights in front and back to welcome evening inspections.

8. Avoid costly renovations. Do not renovate your bathroom or kitchen before you sell your property. The new buyers will look forward to remodeling to their own taste.

9. Have the roof inspected by a qualified company and get a written report as to its condition.

10. Solicit the services of a competent and capable realtor to represent and help you sell your property.

Check List of Things to Do when Purchasing or Selling Your Property

1. Have the property inspected by a competent and qualified building inspector or architect for any defects.

2. Have the property evaluated or appraised based on present day market value.

3. Check survey plan for any irregularities or by-law infractions at the time the survey plan was made, and see whether there have been any additions made since that date. If there are, the plan may have to be updated.

4. Property insurance:
   a) When selling, cancel the policy the day after the closing.
   b) When buying, make sure coverage is for replacement cost of the property. The policy should take effect on the day you purchase the property, which should be confirmed in writing prior to signing the Deed of Sale.

5. Make sure all taxes are paid.

6. Check all items that are included in the sale of the property and make sure all mechanical, plumbing and electrical units such as air conditioners, furnace, pool mechanism, appliances, etc. are in good working order.

7. Mortgage:
   a) When selling, verify and confirm in writing a cancellation option and cost of same, if any.
   b) When buying, have mortgage terms and availability confirmed by lending institution in writing.

8. Utilities must be notified at the time and date of the sale of the property. Read and record the meters as of that date, and keep as reference in case the readings are needed.

9. Obtain a draft copy of the Deed of Sale and adjustment sheet detailing all expenses that are to be incurred and adjusted at the time of sale a few days prior to signing the Deed of Sale.

10. A final physical inspection of the property by the purchaser should be made on or prior to signing the Deed of Sale.

CHAPTER 5

Your Home as an Investment and the Financing that Makes It Happen

If you had purchased a home some 30-odd years ago, chances are you would have seen your $30,000 to $40,000 home grow to an incredible value of $300,000 to $400,000. That kind of growth is an investment worth looking at. Not only was it used as your home but also provided you with a sizable nest egg for retirement. Most of you know the value of owning your own home. If you are one of the lucky ones to have bought that first home many years ago, you have realized a sizable return on your original purchase price. Making that purchase years ago took courage and commitment as well as good money. Well, things haven't changed that much today, apart from the real fact that a starter home today costs a great deal more, and very often both husband and wife must work to pay off their dream home. I hope to show you how you can make this happen, and also save you some problems along the way.

Apart from the fact that most people would like to own their home at some time in their lives, not everyone can afford that dream. The reality is that in order to make that purchase, you must qualify for a mortgage and be able to handle repayment. With the rates of interest as low as they are today, this may be the right time to explore home ownership.

Down Payment

In order to make your initial purchase, you require a down payment to get you started. Some of you are going to tell me you have heard that you can buy a home with no cash. Well, no cash means no responsibility, and the last time I checked, they weren't giving either of them away for free.

Getting that down payment means putting away some money from every pay cheque. This you should be doing anyway, even if you are not planning to buy a home.

A mortgage is the amount you borrow from someone or from an institution like a bank, lending institution or private individual to help you pay for the home you are going to purchase. As you pay it back, in each payment you pay back a small but increasing proportion of capital (the actual cost of the house minus the down payment) plus a declining proportion of the interest on the amount borrowed. Thus, the interest payments are highest at the beginning of the payback period, and the proportion of capital being paid back highest at the end.

In order to qualify for a mortgage, you must first calculate how much of a mortgage you can afford and qualify for. This will also tell you how much of a home you can afford. A rule of thumb is not to spend more than one-third of your total yearly income including your spouse's income, towards the payment of mortgage, taxes, heat, insurance and maintenance. If you have a car loan or personal loan (including your charge card), you would be allowed to use up to 43% of your combined income. Banks and other lending institutions often take your last three years of earnings and average them to arrive at your income level. This allows a better assessment of the amount you would be able to afford to pay on a yearly basis.

If you don't qualify, I suggest you reduce the amount you owe on your charge card or personal loan before you make your application for the mortgage you need. This is the method mortgage companies use to qualify you for a mortgage.

Negotiating the Mortgage

Let's consider a property of $100,000. You have a down payment of $10,000 cash from your savings (I don't recommend that you use all of your savings. You should have set aside some extra cash as rainy day money over and above the amount you put down on the house). A good amount to have put away is six months of monthly payments. This way, in case you lose or change jobs, you will be able to make your mortgage and other payments, so you will not have to worry about making late payments on the house.

Before we go on, I want you to know that making your monthly payments on time is extremely important. It's your lifeline to being creditworthy. Without credit you will have difficulty getting a loan of any kind, let alone a mortgage. Another word of advice: if you are going to have difficulty making a payment on time, always talk to your creditors before the payment is due. They will be very understanding and your foresight will keep you out of the delinquent column. Most monthly mortgage payments are made on a pre-authorized payment plan and therefore are automatically deducted from your bank account. If you don't have the cash to pay for whatever reason, and you don't notify the mortgage lender, the cheque will be deposited and come back NSF, and that means you will have one strike against you. If you notify the lending institution before that happens, they will hold back depositing your cheque until you are able to make the payment.

Having said that, the next big hurdle to climb is how this mortgage you have negotiated is to be paid off and how long it will take. A mortgage loan is very much like any other loan; it has an amortization table telling you what your blended monthly payment, including principal and interest, will be to pay off the loan. Most people borrow money and pay it off over 25 years.

Let's take an example. If you took out a $90,000 mortgage with a fixed annual rate of interest of 8%, and renewal adjustment in five years, your monthly blended capital or principal and interest payment would be $686.89 per month or $8,242.68 per year or up to one third of your combined income.

A good way to save some interest money is not to borrow money over the 25-year term, but rather to pay it off over a shorter period, let's say 20 years instead. The monthly payment for this loan would be $745.52, a difference of $58.63 per month or $703.56 per year. This method would allow you to pay off your loan five years sooner and would save you approximately $27,000 worth of interest payments. Of course if you decided on an even shorter amortization period to pay off your loan, the monthly payments would be slightly higher, but would also save you even more interest in the long term.

Most mortgage and lending institutions allow you to buy down your mortgage, up to 10% of the outstanding balance, once a year, usually on the anniversary date, without a penalty, or you can ask to have the amortization rate lowered by one or two years. Whatever amount you can afford to put towards the mortgage now will save you thousands of dollars worth of interest payments down the road, as I've pointed out in the above illustration. So, if you have the money and can afford a higher monthly payment, which one would you choose? I think the choice is obvious.

Mortgage Brokers

You might also consider getting a mortgage broker who knows the ins and outs of this business, someone who knows most of the lenders in the field on a first-name basis. Mortgage brokers are often paid by the lending institution. In some cases, you may have to pay the fee yourself. I would still recommend you do so; the broker will save you both money and time. You will get the best rate available which will probably more than pay for his fee. When applying for a mortgage, be sure and state all the facts concerning your place of work, how long you've been there, where you live, how long you've lived there, how much you earn, if you have established credit and where.

What the lender wants to know is whether you are capable of paying back the loan. The last thing a lender wants to do is repossess your property. There are many reasons why a lending institution doesn't want to take over a property. To begin with, they don't have the staff to manage properties. They don't want the hassle of going to court. They don't like repossessions which could tarnish their reputation as a good lender. Most lending institutions give the borrower ample time and opportunity to make good on the loan, and repossession is a measure of last resort.

Establishing Credit

If you have not established a credit rating, I recommend you do so as soon as possible. One way is to borrow, let's say, $1,000 from a bank. We will call it Bank #1. You could say you need the money as a personal loan for a period of 2 months with the right to pay off the loan anytime without penalty. Once you've borrowed the money you can take the $1,000 to Bank #2 and open a checking account, then place the $1,000 you just borrowed into a guaranteed investment certificate, payable within 30 days with interest at maturity.

At the end of the 30 days you ask Bank #2 to place the principal and the interest earned in the checking account you opened, and write a cheque payable to Bank #1 where you borrowed the $1,000 plus the interest you now owe. You may have to put some money out of your pocket to cover the cheque you're going to make to Bank #1 because the borrowing rate is usually 1.5 to 2% higher than what the bank gives you on your money; that's how they make their money. In any case, it's a very insignificant amount. Now you go to Bank #1 from which you borrowed the $1,000 initially, and pay off the loan with interest 30 days prior to maturity. You would only pay interest on the 30 days and not the 60 days you originally borrowed. So far so good.

Now you go back to Bank #2 in which you opened a checking account and ask for a personal loan of $1,000 for 90 days. You now take the money and bring it to Bank #1 where you originally borrowed from, and place the money in a guaranteed investment certificate for 60 days. After the 60 days you pay off the loan, again 30 days prior to maturity. You now have established credit with 2 banks for $1,000 each. You can repeat this process for as long as you want, increasing the amount each time you borrow.

You will be amazed at how easily you will be able to get credit once you've established yourself as being credit-worthy. This process will cost you some out-of-pocket money, but the cost involved is insignificant compared to the benefits and rewards you gain as a result of having established credit. When you really come down to it, we now use credit in just about everything we do, whether it's renting or owning your own home or apartment or buying a car. Having a credit rating can help you in the process.

One of the most important ways of maintaining good credit is not to write an NSF cheque. Whenever you do, your bank records this and passes on the information to people who call your bank to check on your credit rating.

By the way, you can always have access to your credit information from your local credit office which will provide you with a detailed report of your credit status. If you see irregularities or things that aren't correct, you should bring them to their attention and have them corrected.

Fees

When applying for a high-ratio mortgage, that is to say an amount higher than 75% of the appraised value or purchase price, whichever is lower, you may incur additional costs which are often overlooked. The lending institution may charge a one-time fee, a small percentage of the loan amount, to cover the cost of insuring the lender against default by the borrower. In the event of a default by the borrower, the lending institution will get its money back and the insurance company will repossess the property.

Other fees which are often overlooked are inspection or appraisal costs and application fees. These items can and should be negotiated or waived at the time of the application. Try to identify all the costs which you will incur during the life of the mortgage, state them in writing, negotiate the terms and state clearly in the contract that there are no additional charges other than the ones identified. Get everyone to sign to that effect, and you will definitely sleep a lot easier and not have to deal with annoying surprises.

Try to determine what the penalty would be in case of prepayment. In most cases, three months worth of interest is the norm; however you should not assume this to be the case. The mortgage agreement should specifically state what the prepayment penalty is going to be before you sign on the dotted line.

Transferring the Mortgage

One thing you should consider doing is agreeing that, in the event you sell your home, the purchaser would have to qualify should he or she want to assume the loan in place on your property. Otherwise, in the case of default by the purchaser, the lender may come after you to recover any loss.

In some cases, you may be able to transfer the mortgage you have from your present home to the home you are going to purchase. The lender may even pick up the cost of transferring the mortgage to the new property, assuming you've maintained your payments on time and are considered a good client. When you have a good credit rating, you can pick and choose your lender and negotiate very favorable terms.

When your credit rating is not so good, the terms of the loan are very often negotiated and dictated for you. In almost all cases where a high-ratio loan is made, the borrower is asked to prepay all the taxes for the following year, up front, or on a monthly basis before they come due, to the lender, along with the monthly principal and interest payment. This is the lender's guarantee that all the taxes are going to be paid on time without interest, and that the mortgage will not be foreclosed because of non-payment of taxes.

For those of you with conventional loans, that is to say mortgage amounts of less than 75% of appraised value or purchase price, you don't have to pay the taxes on a monthly basis to the lender, nor do you have to pay the lender's insurance fee in case of default.

The Real Estate Market and Equity in Your Home

One thing you must consider is that in the event the market price on homes starts to fall, so too does your equity on your home. When this happens, lenders can become panicky. As a result, when your mortgage comes up for renewal, the lender may ask you to buy down the loan by the amount the market has dropped in value. This very issue has caused a flood of homes to be abandoned and repossessed by lending institutions. The borrower no longer has any equity and in some cases the houses are worth less than the outstanding mortgage. Sometimes trying to keep the house and buy down the mortgage is like trying to keep afloat a sinking ship. Everyone believes the prices of homes will keep going higher and higher until the bottom falls out of the market. When people lose their jobs, they also lose the sense of security that comes with having one, and this uncertainty weakens their commitment to buying a home.

Just remember, one man's loss is another's opportunity, so you should always keep an open mind. When people sell, you buy, and when people buy, you sell. It's easy to say, but hard to do because you go against the flow of things. Taking a risk is what life is all about. I've done it all my life. People say that they wish they could have done what I did and keep on saying it. The difference is, successful people do it while others just watch on the sidelines and talk about it.

CHAPTER 6

Other Residential Investment Alternatives

Leasing or Buying a Residential Condominium

Owning a condo is not for everyone. However, many couples, and singles too, have chosen to live in this kind of lifestyle and are quite happy doing so. This arrangement is new to North America and offers many alternatives to the ever-changing needs of today's population. Throughout other parts of the world, this form of housing ownership is not a novelty. In fact it has been a way of life for centuries. The concept of owning air space above and next to each other is both complex and yet so practical that it's hard to imagine how we did without it for so long.

Very often condos are created to meet a demand on the part of a select few who wish to locate in a certain spot. Those who can and want to purchase their unit in a condo complex that has many functional and recreational features and facilities as well as privacy very often find comfort in knowing that they can come and go as they please without having to worry about the upkeep and maintenance of the property. This in itself provides peace of mind for those who are unable to carry out the daily chores of keeping the place orderly and functional, and allows them to enjoy life without worry.

Many people who first purchased their condo unit years ago have probably realized a sizable profit over the course of time. However, current economic developments along with lack of demand have caused prices to tumble in some areas. Recent statistics suggest that in some places throughout North America, the supply outstrips demand by more than 20-1. I believe this to be a short-lived situation; supply and demand will correct themselves over time, especially in heavily populated retirement community markets where the demand is going to grow. This is probably the only market segment where real estate will have a significant growth rate, because of the increase in demand from empty nesters to locate in recreational condo projects.

Owning your own unit requires careful analysis of all technical and legal aspects. Not all condo projects follow the same guidelines and procedures of ownership. I recommend consulting a specialist in your area who can provide you with up-to-date information on both the legal and market situation. Before buying, you should visit several projects to compare prices, location and facilities along with the age and present condition of the units. You should pay special attention to the condo fees.

Condo fees, which are paid on a monthly basis, are based on a combination of expenses, including all forms of taxes (real estate, water, insurance, etc.), regular maintenance such as repairs to all common areas (roof, outside walls, structure, passages, lobby, garage) and upkeep of the grounds all year round, plus the cost of administration to oversee these functions. A historical list of expenses for the past two to four years should be requested and reviewed in order to get a bearing on the consistency and accuracy of the present and future cost estimates.

Before making up your mind to buy a condo unit, you may want to lease to try it out. If that option is available to you, I would recommend that you do it. This kind of lifestyle is not for everyone, and leasing may be a better option at this time, especially if you plan to move around a lot. In some cases it may be easier to pick up the cost of canceling a lease rather than having to sell a condo unit.

One thing is certain. When leasing a condo, you would not have to pay the monthly condo fees which can vary from year to year. If you consider the cost of owning a unit which would include interest on money invested (equity) and your monthly mortgage cost as well as the condo fees, and compare the two on a monthly basis, very often leasing comes out on top by a wide margin!

Looking at it from yet another prospective, leasing may become a better option where market prices have fallen dramatically. Since the people who own condos may not be able to sell them, their second option is to lease them out. You may find that the actual cost of leasing is a lot less than the cost of ownership, and you get to keep your money in a bank earning interest to offset your rent. Remember, money is mobile; real estate isn't. Before you park your money somewhere, consider all your options and then make your move.

As you can see, I've not covered all the pros and cons of condo living with regard to contractual agreements. The reason for this is because they vary from place to place and from developer to developer. Consequently, what works in one place doesn't necessarily work in another location or part of the country. I cannot emphasize enough the importance of getting good expert advice before undertaking such a purchase. Knowing all the rules of the game is a must and a prerequisite in this case. As the legal beagles often say, "Govern yourself accordingly." It really does apply to ownership of a condo unit.

I've seen disappointed people getting the facts about condo agreements—often after the fact. These discrepancies could have been dealt with and corrected before purchasing the unit. A word to the wise—an ounce of prevention is worth a pound of cure. Let this be your guide!

Timesharing

Does it make any sense to buy into a timesharing resort? This oft-asked question has a multitude of answers. Certainly the developers think so, and why not? The mark-up on these properties is astounding! However, timesharing does have merit. It's a bit like owning a condo, only instead of owning the same unit in the complex year after year, you own the unit for one week (or more) of the year, year after year. Timesharing is an option that can fit the budgets of many people. Depending on the exchange network the resort belongs to, you may also be able to exchange your week for a week in another resort in another part of the world. At best, it is a convenient way of setting money aside for that special getaway destination, freezing the cost of doing so at today's rate.

The timeshare package you choose to purchase should be able to be traded with other places of destination of equal, greater or lower value, and the network exchange should be able to adjust the cost, if any, to the value of your unit.

After a closer evaluation, you will note that you have to pay a yearly maintenance and tax fee as part of the cost of ownership. Once you know the total annual cost, including capital and interest of your mortgage (if you have one), as well as the value of your money which is parked there, you can determine whether or not it will be worthwhile to purchase a one- or possibly two-week time period.

Assuming you are going to buy a one-week vacation time slot, you should choose a location and time period that is in demand (usually red weeks have the highest exchange value). Some periods are more in demand than others, even though they may cost the same initially. Be sure to obtain enough information on the developers and the exchange network of which the project is part. See if they have a good track record. Ask to speak to other owners and see what they have to say about their purchase. Find out if they are satisfied **before** you decide to buy a unit.

Sometimes these same people may want to sell their one-week unit at a reduced price, compared to the price at which the developer is offering a unit. Local realtors as well as the exchange network also have lists of units for sale in other resort complexes around the world.

You may be surprised to learn the number of network destinations available in this lucrative business. Next time you travel to a resort destination, why not try renting a unit that is part of a time-sharing program. The rental rates are very often more attractive than what hotels charge. These resorts are very well-maintained and offer a multitude of conveniences right at your doorstep. Whenever I travel, I try to stay in a time-share resort. By the way, don't purchase a unit on your first visit—give yourself time to check it out first.

CHAPTER 7

Real Estate Investments to Meet Your Specific Needs

I've always believed that real estate investments should be made-to-measure to one's lifestyle and portfolio. With that in mind, I will try to illustrate the many types of investments one can make, as well as try to show you how these can be achieved without too much difficulty.

First Time Buyers

Many individuals who have decided to take the plunge and make a real estate investment for the first time are drawn to properties that have a dual purpose. As well as providing shelter for themselves, some properties are income-generating. People who consider this option definitely need some entrepreneurial qualities and should be handy or have available someone who is ready to act on their behalf. Owning a real estate investment requires patience, foresight and good administrative qualities.

The type of work that provides your principal source of income is also a consideration in deciding whether or not you should be making this type of investment. For example, if you travel a lot, or cannot make time available to meet the demands often imposed by a revenue property, chances are this may not be a good idea, nor will it become a good investment vehicle for you. However, if you qualify and are ready to make that decision, here's what you need to do.

Owning a real estate property of any kind requires maintenance from time to time. So you should carefully consider what you can or cannot repair by yourself and then solicit the service of the professionals you will need. If you are not a handyman, you definitely should get one. This individual can save you a lot of money in both labor and material replacement cost.

Next, you will need the services of a roofer, a plumber and an electrician to complete your list. When you are calling these professionals, try to get references, and always have a backup in case one is not available to do the job. Roofers, plumbers and electricians should be on call 24 hours a day. Very often when a problem happens in these three areas, it doesn't give you much warning. When an emergency occurs, you'll feel better knowing that you can react immediately with one phone call **and** trust the troubleshooter you call. Being prepared to act on a moment's notice is a sign of a good professional administrator. A word of advice: preventive maintenance can be the best source of comfort. It can make the difference between acting out of emergency and necessity, or having the time to plan the work at your convenience.

The next step is to find the right real estate investment which best suits your needs. Location is very important. Most real estate investments should be able to support themselves and provide a return on capital invested. By this, I mean the revenue produced by the property should provide adequate income to pay for the expenses incurred, without your having to dip into your pocket every year because the property has become a drain on your bank account.

The Duplex

As an example, we are going to look at an investment which first-time buyers often consider to meet a specific need: the duplex. This type of property is often built on a street that accommodates both single and double dwellings. A duplex has two units, often side-by-side, with a common dividing fire wall, or up and down units where land costs are higher.

With so many people being laid off or caught in company downsizing because of cutbacks, many people are starting their own businesses and often operate out of their home office. In some cases, when zoning permits, owning a duplex becomes an ideal investment, and a place to work from for many types of operation.

To begin with, you should look for this type of property in an area where demand is good and prices are stable. To insure this, the property should be located close to schools, libraries, places to shop, and should have adequate public transportation as well as easy access to major routes. Obviously the closer the property is located to the central core of a city, the higher the demand will be and the higher the price.

Having said that, the next step is to find out how much rent you can afford to pay. Since you are going to live there, you have to pay half the rent which will support half the cost of property as well.

Financing Your Purchase of a Duplex

The unique feature about owning a duplex is the fact that every month you receive a rent cheque to help you pay off the property. Increases in cost of operation and maintenance as well as taxes, interest on mortgages and insurance can be offset and justified by increasing the monthly rental income. A duplex can have both units leased out and provide a source of revenue to supplement income or you can choose to occupy one of the units.

In order to illustrate the cost and maintenance of such a property, we will assume that both units will be leased out. Most duplexes have three bedrooms, a living room, a kitchen, one or two bathrooms and a full basement. In our example, these units are located side-by-side, sometimes referred to as semi-detached. The rental income from each unit is $750.00 per month. Each of the tenants pays his own heating and electrical costs, as well as outside maintenance such as grass cutting and snow removal. The landlord pays all the property taxes except water tax which is individually metered to each unit and billed on consumption.

The rule of thumb is that the purchase price for this type of duplex should not exceed 100 times the monthly rental value. In this case, therefore, the purchase price should not be more than $150,000. This can be misleading in cases where demand is very high or very low, and is meant as a guide and not a rule. Each property should be evaluated, based on its own merits of location and income as well as the potential. I would like to point out that potential is something you should not have to pay for, but is there to be exploited by the purchaser, as an incentive for someone to purchase.

In our example, you should also know that the rent paid each month by the tenants should be the average rent of similar units in the immediate area of where this property is located. If the rent on your property is much higher and it is not justified, then you should make your calculations based on rent the market will bear. In fact, it's better to charge a bit less than the average rent. This way you can rent faster, to individuals you choose, who best suit the property and will maintain the dwelling in good order and maybe not move every year. Landlords often make the mistake of trying to get the highest rent possible, and this often leads to attracting a less stable clientele which moves frequently, which in turn requires you to invest more time and money to redecorate every time a tenant moves.

The following chart illustrates the way you should approach a statement of income and expenses in order to determine value and return of investment.

ANNUAL EXPENSES PAID BY LANDLORD

Real estate taxes (annual)	$1,550.00
Insurance (100% of replacement cost for all risk policy including rental income)	600.00
Maintenance cost (should be 5-6% of yearly income)	900.00
TOTAL:	$3,050.00

MORTGAGE & COST OF PROPERTY

Cost of the Property

Purchase price:	$150,000.00
Cash down payment:	- 40,000.00
Amount of mortgage:	$110,000.00

Cost of the Mortgage

Mortgage: $110,000.00

At a rate of 8% interest per annum, amortized over 20 years and due in 5 years:

Monthly payment of principal and interest:	911.20
Annual cost of mortgage:	$10,934.40

SUMMARY OF ANNUAL REVENUE & EXPENSES

	EXPENSES	REVENUE
Total income: $750.00 per unit per month (2 x $750) x 12 =		$18,000.00
Total expenses:	$ 3,050.00	
Total mortgage payment $911.20 per month x 12 +	10,934.00	
Total Annual Expenses:	$13,984.00	

NET REVENUE:

(Total income–Total expenses) $ 4,016.00

This chart shows you the breakdown of all expenses you should be aware of, which, by the way, should be carefully scrutinized upon inspection of the property. The 5 to 6% maintenance allowance should always be used to calculate unforseen expenses which may not happen every year, but it should be set aside as rainy day money in case of major structural repair, i.e. the roof. You will also notice that the mortgage was amortized over 20 years. That means that in 20 years the property is paid for, if you've kept up the payments on a declining basis. The rent that you receive is paying off the property, leaving you a nice annual return on your initial investment, and a sizeable nest egg to retire on.

As I started to show you at the beginning of this chapter, the cost of owning your own income property is supported by the same rent you would have to pay if the property was leased out. In this case, this is $750 per month plus heating and electrical costs. To make your own evaluation of whether you can afford to live in this property, you should calculate the monthly expenses of rent, taxes, insurance and heating cost. This total should not be more than 32% of your total gross income. This is in line with the standards used by mortgage companies to determine if you can afford the payments on the mortgage. This type of investment requires consideration of all of these issues.

Both personal and financial commitments must not be compromised, otherwise this ideal investment opportunity can become a burden and you will suffer losses you did not anticipate. You must plan carefully and the goal must sit well with your expectations and realities. There's an old saying: If you don't plan, you plan to fail. Heed these words of wisdom and you will always be one step ahead of the problem.

Insurance

You may have noticed in my illustrations that the insurance is for 100% coverage. This means that you should be insured at all times for 100% of the present day replacement cost. In order to determine this, you should get the property appraised and be sure of what the figure is. However, most insurance companies and brokers know the approximate amount of replacement cost and they multiply it by the number of square feet of the property and, voilà, the replacement cost of the property.

Here is a more detailed example. Let's say your property has dimensions of 30'x 40', is a single story plus an unfinished basement. We are going on the assumption that the replacement cost is $100 per square foot. We know that the house is 1,200 sq. ft.

Replacement Cost

EXAMPLE & METHOD OF CALCULATION

House 30 x 40 = 1,200 sq. ft.
Replacement cost (living area)
$100.00 sq. ft. X 1 200 sq. ft. = $120,000.00
Unfinished Basement = 1 200 sq. ft.
Replacement cost
$50.00 X 1,200 sq. ft.
or half cost of the finished area   60,000.00
                                        _____

                                                $180,000.00

The total replacement cost of your property is determined by the cost factor of both floors. As you may have noticed in my examples, the basement is not finished and therefore has less value than the upper floor.

In our example of the duplex, if you live in one of the units, the rate of insurance charged is going to be less than what you would pay for a unit which is rented out. So your overall rate will be lower. Insurance companies offer a discount on any revenue property which is owner-occupied. I should also mention that mortgage lenders give a preferred lending rate to owner-occupied revenue properties as opposed to revenue-producing properties which are not occupied by the landlord.

A word of caution, and this is very important...If one or more units are unoccupied, you must notify the insurance company. You will have to physically inspect the empty unit every day, otherwise, in case of a loss, the insurance company will not pay the coverage stipulated in the policy.

Whenever you insure a property and you have a mortgage, the lender will ask you to place a clause in the policy that, in the event of a loss, the lender will be paid because he has prior claim. This is quite normal and any small claim will not have any effect on this clause. However, in a major loss or total destruction, the insurance company is bound by this clause to pay the lender as well as you, in which case if you want to rebuild, the funds will be used from the proceeds of the claim. That's the reason why mortgage lenders want a copy of the insurance policy and its renewal to ensure that adequate coverage is maintained at all times.

When placing insurance, get coverage for all risks and read the policy carefully. Most people only read the insurance policy when they have a claim, only to discover they cannot claim because the policy did not cover the incident. Most insurance policies require a lawyer to understand them, because they were written by a lawyer. Some insurance companies have now decided to rewrite these policies in plain language so that everyone can better understand about what is and what is not covered. I would sometimes read one paragraph and think I was covered, only to find, on further reading, that there were three or four reasons why the company would not pay for such a loss.

If you are not clear on the wording in your policy, ask your broker to explain it to you and get it in writing from the insurance company if you need to, to be absolutely certain what it is they are saying. Don't settle for less. It is because people have been asking for clearer definitions of what they are responsible for that the insurance companies are making changes to the wording of their policies.

When you have rental income property, be sure to get coverage that will pay the rent in case of a loss. This type of insurance is called rental income insurance. You will still have bills to pay, and it will be a relief to know that you will be able to meet these obligations in the event that your property is damaged and tenants are not paying rent until the property is restored to its original state and condition.

I've tried to cover all the issues which may be of concern when purchasing a revenue-producing property of 2 to 5 units, to give you a better perspective of what to expect. I hope you will bear in mind these concerns if you decide to purchase a revenue property. The secret to success with a small property like this is your attitude, and, as a friend once told me, your attitude will ultimately determine your altitude.

Apartment Building (6-12 units)

Another type of investment, which requires a little more attention and is well suited to the intermediate investor, is the 6-to 12-unit apartment building. This property requires supervision on a daily basis. People who usually purchase these kinds of properties are handymen of all types and trades, who are often capable of doing most of the required maintenance.

The Role of Tenant-Administrator

Access corridors to the individual units must be kept clean and accessible at all times, a daily chore. That is why I recommend that you appoint one of the tenants to handle this responsibility along with changing light bulbs, clearing snow or cutting grass, as well as showing prospective tenants the units that are available for rent. In some cases, you can also make this person responsible for collecting rent cheques every month.

The administrator-tenant should be paid in accordance with his level of responsibility and capacity to handle these functions. To some degree, he is handling functions on behalf of the landlord and therefore should be courteous and have good administrative skills. If you are able to offer your tenants an individual who can handle routine functions on a daily basis, you will be rewarded immeasurably. You will have satisfied tenants (you should view them as your clients in the real sense of the word; it will give you a different prospective in your relationship with them), and your clients will feel reassured that in case of an emergency, there is someone they can turn to. This individual can also deflect tension which sometimes arises because of a misunderstanding between tenant and landlord.

Financing

The most often asked question about these types of properties is how much should I pay for them. To best answer the question it is necessary to know the location, condition, demand for and the availability of such a property. Ultimately this will always depend on what the bottom line shows. By this I mean, what is left after all the expenses are paid for. The expenses are often underrated. A true understanding of what they are, is essential for a well-informed decision to invest or not, is the basis for negotiation over what the selling price should be. You may have heard about the rule of thumb, "6 x 8 x revenue" or price per unit and so on. All of this means absolutely nothing if there is no money left to pay yourself for the cash investment you have made after all the expenses have been accounted for.

Return on Investment

A management fee as well as an equitable return on your cash investment should be the minimum return you should settle for. If you don't approach these types of investment in this way you may find yourself overworked and underpaid as the saying goes, as well as being frustrated when the going gets tough, as it sometimes does. We will look at a typical property and review all the financial aspects of the revenue and income statement.

As our example, we are going to use an 8-unit walk-up apartment. In our case the tenants pay their own heating costs, electricity, and water tax. Common area heating and electrical costs are paid by the landlord, and the landlord supplies a refrigerator and stove in each unit. Our property is located on the fringe of a single-family dwelling neighborhood, near light industry and commercial properties, has bus transportation within easy walking distance and is accessible to major transportation routes within minutes from the site. The property is in a good state of repair, has been well looked after, and the rents are all average rents when compared to other buildings in the immediate area. (A careful analyses of neighboring similar type and size properties should always be carried out prior to submitting an offer on the property.)

The owner is selling because he is getting on in years and does not want the responsibility of looking after a place any longer. The property has been placed for sale with an asking price of $225,000.

REVENUE & EXPENSES STATEMENT

	Revenue
6 units 4 rooms $350.00 per month	$ 2,100.00
2 units 3 rooms $275.00 per month	550.00
8 units	$2,650.00
Revenue $2,650.00 Per month x 12 =	$31,800.00

	Expenses
*Taxes (real estate and others)	$4,700.00
*Heat and electricity (common areas)	900.00
*Insurance (all risk and rental loss)	650.00
Administration fee of 5% (of total gross income) you pay yourself	1,908.00
Vacancy (5% of gross income)	1,590.00
Advertising and promotion	500.00
Maintenance (5% of gross income)**	1,590.00
*Janitor (caretaker) $150.00 per month	1,800.00
TOTAL EXPENSES: (for the year)	$13,638.00

* All these expenses should be carefully verified as to their accuracy, and guaranteed by the vendor as being true and accurate to the best of his knowledge.

** If this amount is not used in the course of 1 year, the remaining balance should be set aside in case of major expense like a new roof and so on.

SUMMARY

Total Revenue:	$31,800.00
Total Expense:	13,356.00
	————
Balance After Expenses:	$18,444.00

Let us now determine the price to pay for such a property in order for us to achieve a 12% return on cash invested, after paying off our mortgage. We are going to apply for a conventional mortgage and place at least 25% of the purchase price as a cash down payment on a property. We also know that we want to purchase this property and keep it at least 5 years. So we are going to apply for a mortgage that has a rate of interest of 8% per annum, compounded semi-annually and amortized over a 20-year period; and comes due in five years. Our down payment is going to be $50,000 cash at the signing of the Deed of Sale. The rest of the money needed to pay the vendor off in full will be borrowed from a lending institution. Since we are looking at a 12% return on our cash investment, the sum of $6,000 must be set aside from the balance of revenue.

Balance of Revenue After Expenses:		$18,444.00
Cash Investment Return:	$50,000.00 x 12%	$ 6,000.00
Balance:		$12,444.00

We know that the amount of $12,444.00 is what is left to pay off a loan of an amount to be determined. As we stated, the mortgage rate for a 5-year loan is 8% and the amortization term is 20 years. With this information we can turn to amortization tables and see how much money we can borrow and pay off with the balance of the $12,444 left over after all other expenses have been paid.

When dividing our balance by 12 we are able to find out how much we can pay per month towards the capital and interest. In this case it will be $1,037.00 per month. If we look at the amortization table of 20 years at 8% per annum, we can see that the amount which corresponds most closely to the $1,037 is $1,014.93, which would be the amount paid monthly for capital and interest payment to amortize a loan of $150,000.00.

Our illustration has shown us that we can easily afford a mortgage loan of $150,000.00 and pay off all our necessary expenses, and leave a 12% rate of return on our cash investment of $50,000.00.

1st mortgage loan	$150,000.00
Cash invested	50,000.00
TOTAL PURCHASE PRICE:	$200,000.00

In conclusion, we can afford to pay up to $200,000 for this property or 6.28 times the revenue. Another way of looking at it is that the expenses (not including the mortgage payment) are 42.8% of gross income. Some will argue that the percentage allotted for expenses on a tenant-heated apartment building is far too high. However the fact remains that all of the expenses outlined are not prefabricated but are actually realistic and necessary. One of the main reasons why some landlords cannot operate in the black and have money left over at the end of the year is that they either paid too much for the property in the first place, or did not allow enough money for expenses, which forces them to operate in the red. If they cannot make ends meet, they end up losing the property to the mortgage company and wonder what went wrong.

A purchaser of an investment property who does not use a proven method to determine value and decides to use figures that do not properly reflect that reality will sooner or later face a shortfall he did not count on.

I'm not suggesting my method is the best or the only one to use. However, you should be realistic enough to know that by lowering your estimate of expenses, you may also be lowering your rate of return on investment. As the saying goes, you can take care of it now or you can pay for it later; the choice is yours. My reasoning is simple: the cost of doing business in the real estate world is always going up, and if we want to stay in business, we either have to raise rents or cut costs. If you don't make the proper assessment of the expenses, you may have to do both. In today's economy, one thing is certain: taxes are definitely going up and the successful investor will consider all the options before raising rents and risking having an apartment empty, without collecting any rent at all and having to pay all the expenses anyway.

As I am writing this book, the so-called experts are still trying to figure out what went wrong with the real estate industry in the '90s. Investors and developers all over North America play the blame game, trying to find excuses for how things went wrong, and blame something or someone else for their shortcomings. While banks and lending institutions lost billions of dollars, these same institutions have lost confidence in the real estate market. They now shy away in droves where before they were competing for positions in a losing game. The hammer had to fall, and hard it did fall on everyone who did not play by the proven rules. They played "pretend" until reality set in and everything came tumbling down.

Well, this is the way we are going to do business in the new real estate world. We are going back to basics and if you don't like the rules you won't be allowed to play the game any more. Once the banks and lending institutions learn how to lend money again, they will come to realize that real estate is still the safest and most dependable commodity to invest in. The demand for real estate will increase, which in turn will bring back stability to a market that was destined for doom with no hope of ever making a comeback. Hard-hit investors should cut their losses and get on with their lives and learn from the experience. It doesn't mean you should leave the real estate business. On the contrary, you are now that much wiser and will be a guardian of the new rules, and as well, have the ability to validate your new-found knowledge and build on a much stronger base.

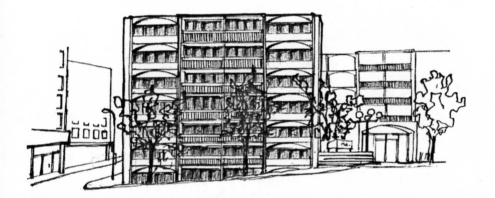

CHAPTER 8

Revenue Properties: 12 Units and Over

Some of the best real estate investment opportunities that have turned to disasters are properties of 12 or more units. By this I mean that landlords who failed as good property managers have turned good quality property investments into neglected slums. There is an expression often used for this type of individual: "They have milked the cow to its last drop…" They buy properties but don't do necessary or preventive maintenance; keep them for a year or two; then they either try to sell them or end up giving them back to the mortgage company and walking away, leaving behind a trail of bad memories for everyone concerned, not to mention the bad reputation often associated with landlords of these type of properties.

Well, I'm happy to report that these individuals are a small minority in the real estate industry. Unfortunately, they very often make the headlines and get a lot of attention that give the business of real estate ownership a bad name. As I've tried to show you in the previous chapter, one must take precautions when buying such properties. However, you can take the same good administrator of a small 8-unit apartment building, make some corrective adjustments to reflect the increase in responsibility and, voilà, you have a property manager who can take command of an apartment complex. You can address and delegate responsibility and turn these investments into profitable ventures.

Very often, large apartment complexes are owned by a group of individuals who pool their money to buy these properties. The group often hires a property manager to take care of the·day-to-day responsibility of operating a larger building. In some cases you have absent owners who don't even live in the country, yet these properties operate in the black and often enjoy 100% occupancy because the owners have taken the proper steps to make this happen.

There are many benefits to ownership of larger apartment properties. However, unless a properly planned operating budget is drawn up at the time of purchase, this investment opportunity can become your worst nightmare, and cause you to lose the capital you invested. So, to avoid such an experience, we are going to take a close look at the do's and don'ts, and what a good operating budget should look like to properly address the expenses needed to make this investment profitable and successful.

Our example will be an apartment complex of 64 units. This property is a 6-story detached concrete and brick enclosed structure. It has 2 elevators, inside parking spaces for 45 cars and 40 outside parking spaces on the grounds. It is located just off a main road and enjoys access to a public transportation system a short, two-minute walk from the property. The property is located a 10-minute walk or 2-minute drive away from a regional mall.

The 64 units are made up as follows: 4 penthouses; 36 units of 4 ½ rooms; 18 units of 3 ½ rooms; 6 units of 2½ rooms. The property enjoys an enclosed rooftop swimming pool (no supervision), a sauna, and a rooftop lounging area for sun bathers. Coin-operated laundry facilities are provided in the basement next to the garage area, and garbage dispensers are located outside next to the garage exit. A full-time janitor and his wife look after daily cleaning of common areas in the building and grounds, as well as light maintenance work such as changing tap washers, light bulbs, cutting grass, etc. The owners have an agreement with the janitor that he will be paid extra for any required painting, as well as receiving a $25 bonus for each apartment he rents. He enjoys the use of a 3 ½-room unit, rent-free, as well as a weekly salary. Professional tradesmen are called in for any major repair work that is required, and they are available 24 hours a day in case of an emergency.

The building is in a good state of repair, and preventive maintenance is carried out routinely. The landlord supplies heat and hot water to all apartments. Each unit has a thermostat control that regulates the heat coming in and air-conditioning facilities with a designated plug outlet, and a balcony. The landlord supplies a refrigerator and stove at a nominal cost, if required by the tenant.

We now have enough background knowledge to make a decision about acquiring such a property, provided, of course, the price and expenses reflect the true picture of the facts and expectations. In this example, I'm not going to indicate the asking price. We will arrive at the market value of this property by using this proven method. When a property is placed for sale, a similar exercise should be carried out to determine a probable asking price.

A check of rents in neighboring properties should be a priority. A comparison of rents in similar properties and what they offer to attract prospective tenants should be given careful consideration. If the property you are about to make an offer on has rentals that are higher than the norm and these cannot be justified, you may have to increase the vacancy factor from 5% to 6 or possibly 7% in your estimate of costs. In cases where the rents are lower than the average rent in the area, chances are good that tenants are not going to move as often, and the figure of 5% used for vacancy, the norm, is quite acceptable. A sure way to find out how secure the tenants are, is to know how long they have been there. If tenants renew their lease year after year, it means they are comfortable and well looked after.

Often federal government agencies and professional associations in the real estate and housing field provide statistics on vacancies in a given region. This information is free and should be accessed on a regular basis as a point of reference. You may have to compile a lot information to get some very meaningful data. Sometimes you can see trends that are happening or starting to take shape.

Now, we will look at a statement of income and expenses to determine how much money you should pay for this property. Some tenants have their own fridge and stove, some have an inside garage and some pay more than others, but for the sake of simplicity I have averaged the rents by the size of apartments.

REVENUE & EXPENSE STATEMENT

4	Penthouses at $1,100.00 each per month 4 x $1,100.00 =	$ 4,400.00
36	Units of 4 ½ rooms at $750.00 each per month 36 x $750.00 =	27,000.00
18	Units of 3 ½ rooms at $550.00 each per month 18 x $550.00 =	9,900.00
6	Units of 3 ½ rooms at $400.00 each per month 6 x $400.00 =	2,400.00

Total monthly apartment rental:	$ 43,700.00
Yearly apartment rental:	$ 524,400.00
Income from washer and dryer machines:	$ 12,500.00

Total gross rental for the year:	$ 536,900.00

LIST OF EXPENSES

Taxes (all taxes assessed to the property)	$ 48,000.00
Heating and Hot water (oil furnaces)	35,000.00
Insurance (all risk and rental loss coverage)	6,000.00
Electricity (for outside and common areas)	6,500.00
Elevator (yearly service contract)	3,400.00
Janitor (including apartment value)	36,000.00
Management 6% of total rental	32,214.00
Vacancy: 5% of total rental	26,845.00
Maintenance: 6% of total rental (including advertising and promotion)*	32,214.00

Total Expenses for the year :	$ 226,173.00

* A careful evaluation of each unit must be carried out to determine the proper status of the property. The figure of 6% allocated for maintenance is a minimum amount, not a rule, and should be carefully evaluated for each individual property. The older the building, the higher the percentage should be, depending on the level of maintenance of the building.

Additional expenses can be added to this list, such as structural reserve, usually 2-3% of gross revenue, replacement of refrigerators and stoves, etc.

NET BALANCE

Total Yearly Revenue:	$536,900.00
Total Yearly Expenses:	226,173.00
Total Net Rental:	$310,727.00

At this point we have come to realize our net balance after all expenses are paid for. I'd like to discuss some of these expenses from the perspective of a little background knowledge, namely the role of the janitor. (Probably some of you are saying by now, "I want that job! Look at what this guy is going to pay someone to look after his building.") The fact is, this individual has a tremendous responsibility and should be paid well. He can make or break you. You've often heard this phrase and it certainly applies to caretakers of buildings. If you hire the right individual (which is not easy to do unless you pay good wages), you will have a trouble-free property which will not only make a consistent profit year after year, but also be a pleasure to own and keep for a very long time.

On the subject of taxes, as you already know, they can vary from one city to another, depending on the total debt one city has compared to another. Obviously the lower the debt, the smaller the taxes will be. This is very important to know, because the less expense one has on a property of this kind, the higher the net revenue will be, with a justifiably higher value on the property.

Of course this same reasoning applies to all expenses that apply to such properties. For example, installing a more efficient burner on the furnace and hot water tank, thereby reducing your overall cost of operation, will increase your net profit.

In our illustration, we have determined that the amount of $310,727.00 was left after all expenses were paid. In order to purchase this property, we have decided to give $900,000.00 cash, and we would like to achieve a 12% annual return on the cash invested. The owner has indicated that he is able to leave a balance of sale at 8% per annum, payable monthly for a period of seven years, with the right to prepay the amount at any time. There is an existing, transferable mortgage of $1,600,000 which bears interest at 7.75% per year, which comes due in three years. The original mortgage was taken out two years ago and had an amortization of 20 years. If we were to assume it today, it would have 18 years left to go, and this fits in with our plan to have an amortization rate of 20 years or less. Even though the mortgage is transferable to a new buyer, the new purchasers would still have to qualify in order to assume the original mortgage. By this, I mean he or she would require a proven credit record somewhere in order to assume the existing mortgage on the property.

Our strategy here is to assume the existing mortgage of $1,600,000 so our $900,000 cash is sufficient down payment for the owner of the property and the balance of the price would be assumed by him. We know that the present mortgage is due for re-negotiation in three years. We can either have the balance of sale come due at the same time as the first mortgage or we can go beyond that to five years, in which case it would still be advisable to renew the existing mortgage which is coming due three years from now for a period of not more than two years when the balance of sale with the owner becomes due.

The reason for this is probably obvious to you by now. We want the balloon payment to the owner to become due at the same time as the first mortgage; this way we can increase the mortgage by the same amount as the balance owed to the owner-vendor. This way, we will not have to look for a second mortgage or pay the entire sum out of our pocket. In most cases, a balance of sale with the owner-vendor of the property should not be transferable to another buyer. In other words if you, the present buyer, were to sell the property to someone else, even though the present first mortgage clearly states it is transferable, the purchaser would not have to qualify to assume the amount of the balance of sale. Because there is no restriction indicated, if the property were to be sold to another purchaser, the entire amount of the balance of sale would become due automatically and that restrictive clause in the deed, "due on sale," would apply. Another clause should be mentioned in the deed in the event that the present first mortgage of $1,600,000 is increased, let's say by an amount of $200,000, to $1,800,000. The amount by which the first mortgage is increased ($200,000) must be applied to reduce the balance of sale of the previous owner. This will ensure the same quality equity collateral throughout the term of the balance of sale until the entire sum is paid to the owner.

In order to complete our proposal, let's go over what we now know.

First mortgage of $1,600,000.00 at 7.75%

Monthly C & I payment of $13,014.77 x 12 (m) =	$156,177.24
Cash down payment of $900,000.00 12% return on the amount invested: $900,000.00 x 12% =	$108,000.00
Sub total:	$264,177.24

The sum of $310,727 was left after all expenses were paid. After paying the first mortgage, $156,177.24, and allocating $108,000 for our 12% return on money invested, we are left with a balance of $46,549.76. The vendor indicated he would take back a balance of sale at 8% per annum. Knowing this, we can determine the value of $46,549.76 at 8% per annum as being $581,872.00. Therefore the amount becomes a second mortgage with the owner-vendor, and could either become due in three years at the same time as the first mortgage, or possibly in five years. In any case, you should state in the deed that this amount could be paid off in its entirety without penalty at any time throughout the term of the mortgage.

Here I would like to show you how creative financing can allow both purchaser and vendor to have their cake and eat it too. If we lower the interest rate of 8% per annum to 7%, the end value would be $664,996.57 instead $581,872.00. This creates a larger balloon payment at the end of the term. If the vendor wanted to receive a certain price for his property, one way of achieving it would be to reduce the interest on the balance of sale, thereby creating a higher value with $46,549.76 left after all expenses have been paid. When using this method, one should carefully consider the length of time it would take to realize the saving equal to the higher value that has been created.

We will round off the amount to $582,000. In effect we have established a true value of the property based on the interest rates that apply to today's market conditions.

Summary

First Mortgage:	$1,600,000.00
Cash down payment:	900,000.00
Balance of sale:	582,000.00
Total Value:	$3,082,000.00

This is the amount we should pay for the property based on revenue and expenses. Needless to say, if interest rates or general expenses or both were to go up, the price would be lower, and conversely if they were to go down, the price would go up. When you have a vendor who is ready to take back a mortgage on the property such as the one in this illustration, different values can be created to reflect the needs of both purchaser and vendor: that's how the term creative financing came about. You may have heard another expression, "Liars figure but figures don't lie." This is so true when it applies to revenue properties. Unless you are realistic when you create value, you may find yourself on the short end of the stick. Common sense has to prevail for both vendor and purchaser to conclude a quality transaction. If the deal looks good today, it's only because measures have been taken to validate that statement. Very often, unpredictable market conditions can cause concern; this is why when dealing on large properties, long term solutions create stability.

Mortgage Financing

I'll give you an example of how a $6,000,000 mortgage loan should be viewed from my prospective. I would divide the $6,000,000 into three $2,000,000 loans coming due at three different times with the same lending institution, let's say one in one year, one in two years and one in three years. If the rate is high at the time of renewal, you are not affected on the entire sum of $6,000,000 but only on the $2,000,000 which is due. If the rate is low, lock-in for long term and do the same as the others come due. You must do this kind of creative thinking in order to survive and stay in the black.

Whenever someone offers you a property for sale, disregard the asking price. Try applying the formula we have just gone over. If the deal makes sense, negotiate the best possible price without compromising on risk that may mortgage your future and take away the potential of the property. I should point out that there are other methods and strategies one can use to determine value. My example is a simple illustration of one of them.

Additional expenses such as structural reserves, usually 2-3% of gross income, cost of replacement of refrigerators and stoves, mechanical break down, etc. are also used to make up the expense list. Each property should be evaluated individually based on its age, location, the type of tenants that occupy the building, whether the property is properly maintained, etc. All of these factors should be taken into account on the expense list.

CHAPTER 9

Semi-Commercial and Commercial Revenue Properties

Most owners of semi-commercial properties with several business options to exploit, all within the same property and under the same roof, can identify with this type of investment. They can vary in any number of ways, such as locating stores on the lower level and apartments on the top floors. Often these same residential apartments can be turned into offices or another type of commercial activity. In fact, some apartment buildings that have a storefront feature have been completely converted to commercial use, which very often increases revenue and also increases the total value of the property. In all cases, this type of property used for commercial purposes invariably has more value per square foot of construction than a residential use would have.

Commercial space is leased on the basis of a price per square foot. The price charged per square foot is determined by the demand for it in that area. Some commercial leases are either gross or net net. Gross commercial leases may include built-in expenses such as taxes, heat, (in some cases) insurance, etc., management of property and some maintenance, as well as the net effective rent.

In addition, an escalation clause allows the landlord to charge the tenant any increase in these costs pro-rated to the amount of square feet occupied. Some leases are indexed to the cost of living. That means if the cost of living goes up (according to the consumer price index), say by 3%, so too would the rent.

Some landlords' semi-commercial properties, in addition to having an escalation clause, charge the bulk of all expenses to the stores. The reasoning is justified when you consider that the stores use more heat than the residential tenants upstairs, and taxes, insurance and maintenance cost go up as a direct result of the commercial activity. For example, a storefront restaurant can cause insurance on the property to increase dramatically. Having to pay the increase in the cost of the premium would be considered justifiable. So, in effect, if a commercial tenant's activity is a direct cause of the increased insurance cost, he should be responsible for paying for it.

Careful consideration must be given to the type of commercial tenant you choose to occupy your property. Consider how it will affect the other tenants in the building. For example I would not lease to a pet store with noisy animals that would occupy space under a dwelling, unless proper measures have been taken care of, such as sound proofing. I once saw a landlord lease to two different grocery stores in the same building right next to each other. It's obvious the first grocery store didn't do his homework well.

When he leased, he should have required the landlord to give him an exclusivity clause in his lease saying that the landlord could not lease to another grocery store within the same building. The reasoning is obvious. You would think the landlord could have worked this out on his own without having to be told.

When choosing to purchase a semi-commercial property, consider if both residential and commercial tenants can co-exist. Ideally, the residential tenants should have their own unique, separate entrance, preferably located on the side away from the commercial activity. Residential tenants have more sensitive needs and require special care. On the other hand, if you have a commercial property without residential use, both storefront and upstairs entrance can be on the same side as the storefront; in fact, it's advisable. Very often this property contains stores on the ground level and mixed-use offices upstairs.

Again, when buying commercial or semi-commercial property, try to see if the rents are reasonable when compared to other properties in the area. Also consider whether or not the merchants provide useful services and functions which are in demand, so those stores will thrive and continue to occupy space in the property. Most commercial properties that have common access and services are unable to provide separate heating and air conditioning systems or separate electrical meters to monitor individual costs, so the landlord pays for them and charges them back to the tenants on a pro-rated basis. These charges include an allowance for common areas as well. Even though the leases are considered gross in that they include all of the services, any increase to these costs will be charged back to the tenants.

For example, if we signed a gross lease in 1985 for 1645 square feet of office space, including 145 square feet of common area, and the rent was $13.50 per square foot, the annual rent would be $13.50 x 1645 sq. ft. = $22,207.50 divided by 12 = $1,850 per month. The landlord is offering a gross lease for $1,850.00 per month. That price includes taxes, insurance, heat, maintenance, office cleaning (not always included) air conditioning, etc. However, if any of these expenses do go up, the landlord will adjust the rent by using 1985 as the base year. In other words, whatever the amount was in 1985, you would calculate the increased portion and distribute the expense proportionately to the amount of space each tenant occupies.

On the other hand, if a lease is net net, the tenant pays a base rent plus whatever the expenses are, on a monthly basis. This type of lease covers in greater detail the list of expenses the tenant is responsible for. Most net leases outline the expenses as being everything that requires maintenance, replacement and upkeep, except for the structure of the building, which the landlord is responsible for.

Contracts

Purchasing a commercial or semi-commercial property requires a little more talent and savvy than buying your average residential property. Most residential properties have what is known as a "standard lease form," with only small variations from lease to lease. Commercial leases are a little more intricate and require fine-tuning by lawyers to address the necessary legal concerns. They are in most cases filled with legal beagle terminologies that could be less complicated and made much easier to understand without having to consult a lawyer each time you have to look up what you signed for.

The basic issue is this: how many square feet of space do I need to rent? How much is the rent? How long is the lease? And we know that if the lease is net, the tenant pays for everything including the kitchen sink. That's all there is to it, and it all should be said on one sheet of paper which two people can sign, understand and agree on in a matter of minutes. However, lawyers are now involved and these leases have to be scrutinized by them before signing.

Because of this, when you are submitting a written offer to purchase, it should always be stated in the offer, that "the purchaser has the right to peruse and approve all leases until he or she is completely satisfied with same, otherwise the offer to purchase and its acceptance would become null and void without recourse by either party." This clause or a similar one should be used to address the concerns for clarification of the commercial leases at all times, without exception.

My next concern is to specify in the offer to purchase exactly what the lease says. This covers the square footage, the rent (net or gross), term of lease, options (if any) and who pays for what. More importantly, it specifically states that the owner-vendor guarantees this along with all expenses and revenues to be true and exact. It should also state that any verbal agreement made by the landlord and the tenants will not be honoured by you unless specifically stated in writing and approved by you with your signature.

As you can see, these types of properties require more technical work and legal preparation in order to satisfy the concerns that one may have when purchasing such a property.

Mortgage Financing

One other issue I would like to deal with is borrowing for a commercial property. Lending institutions use a higher rate to determine expenses for this type of property, and very often lend only up to 60% of the value to get a conventional mortgage rate. In fact, the rate charged on commercial properties is often higher than that on residential units. What this means is that you either must have 40% of the purchase price in cash or get the vendor to give you a balance of sale on the difference between your cash deposit and the amount required to finalize the sale.

Determining Value

In order to determine how much you should pay for such a property, we are going to use as our example three properties to illustrate their unique differences and the application of proven methods that help to maintain stability and provide good management skills.

Example 1

Our first example is a semi-commercial corner property, with four stores, located on the main road, 12 walk-up apartments on 2 floors fronting on a side street, and its own private entrance. The property is approximately 25 years old, is semi-detached, in an area which is almost 100% built up, with little or no vacant land available for development. It is located in a community five miles from a major city center. Most stores in these areas have stood the test of time and weathered the storms of newer, bigger and better regional shopping malls that have opened up and may now be on the verge of closing. (That's another story, which I will deal with at length in another chapter).

The grocery and butcher store is a "mom and pop" shop which is a thriving business. Its niche is that it sells special select cuts of meat, prepares cold cuts and cheeses and imports European lines of grocery items. It has been there since the building was constructed. It occupies 3,000 sq. ft. plus the basement.

Next to it is a barber shop, and that tenant too has been there since the property was built. The barber shop occupies 500 sq. ft. Next to the barber is a flower shop which sells freshly cut flowers and arrangements for all occasions. It has been there for 12 years, and occupies 1000 sq. ft.

Next to the flower shop is a dry cleaner which also does alterations. It has been operating for 15 years and occupies 1000 sq. ft. All stores have the use of their basement except for the barber who has given up his space to the adjacent grocery store. If you said you would bank on these stores to do well, your first impression would be absolutely correct.

Next we are going to look at the status of the upstairs apartments. These are 6 units of 4 ½ rooms, and 6 units of 3 ½ rooms making up the 12 units. They are all leased on a yearly basis and the landlord supplies the heat and pays all taxes including water, which is metered for the entire building. The apartments have never been updated since actual construction, and although they have been well taken care of, wear and tear and age have taken their toll. They need upgrading, which is one of the reasons the landlord wants to sell. He has realized his dream; he bought the property 25 years ago, got a closed amortized mortgage for 25 years, has paid it off completely, and now wants to place his money in a retirement fund. He would have to make a major investment to upgrade the units. He is wise not to carry out such an undertaking; by allowing a new owner to come in and make this kind of major renovation to his own liking, he also gives the purchaser an incentive to buy this property, exploit the potential of more revenue and increase the value of the property.

The roof was replaced 5 years ago and has a transferable 10-year written guarantee with a roofing company that's been in business for the last 30 years. The wooden windows are original and the outside double hung windows have been replaced by new white enamel aluminum windows, which are in good shape. The property has a good quality clay brick covering with recessed joints, and doesn't require pointing or replacement. The furnace is an original, sectional, cast-iron unit which has a modern, 2-year-old, 85% efficient oil burner. The burner has 3 years left on the guarantee which is also transferable to the new owner.

The owner has a handyman who lives 2 doors away to look after the property on a daily basis as well as do all the minor repairs that are needed.

Our interest is to determine the value of such a property and submit an offer to purchase to the vendor for his consideration. We know that the owner has paid off the mortgage. He has indicated that he may take back a small balance of sale for 5 years at current market rates or at the same rate that we would pay for a new first mortgage.

Revenue and Expense Statement

On all residential leases, the rents have been standardized for the sake of simplicity.

Revenue-Residential Units

6 units of 4 ½ rooms each at $475.00 per month 6 x $475.00 =	$2,850.00
6 units of 3 ½ rooms each at $350.00 per month 6 x $350.00 =	2,100.00
Sub total:	$4,950.00

The commercial leases have been in place for more than five years each, and, rather than go back and find out what the base rent was when each of the leases took effect, I've simply calculated what the base rent was five years ago and added all the increases that have taken place since then. It is understood in my example that the stores pay 66% of all the expenses of the property which exceed the base year rate.

Revenue-Commercial Leases

PLACE	% SPACE occupied	SQ.FT. sq. ft.	RENT per month	PRICE per sq. ft.	YRS. LEFT on lease	OPTION
Grocery Store	55%	3,000	$3,750.00	$15.00	5 years	5 years
Barber Shop	9%	500	750.00	$18.00	5 years	5 years
Flower Shop	18%	1,000	1,375.00	$16.50	3 years	2 x 5 yrs.
Dry Cleaner	18%	1,000	1,375.00	$16.50	5 years	2 x 5 yrs.
		5,500	$7,250.00			

REVENUE SUMMARY

Monthly Rental of Apartments:	$ 4,950.00
Monthly Rental of Stores:	$ 7,250.00
Total Monthly Income:	$12,200.00

The gross commercial rents were based on the expenses of five years ago. Included were taxes, insurance and heat, which totalled $36,200. In effect, the stores would pick up 66% of any increase over this figure, and pay the landlord in the form of a recovery over and above the rent which was established five years ago. These leases do not cover maintenance costs, management fees or janitorial expenses as they do not apply and the leases were not structured that way.

EXPENSES FOR THE YEAR[2]

Taxes *	$25,359.00
Heating *	9,765.00
Insurance*	3,312.00
(Including rental insurance and all risk)	
Maintenance (approx. 5% of gross income)	7,320.00
Management (6% of gross income)	8,784.00
Vacancy rate (5% of gross income)	7,320.00
Janitor ($500.00 per month)	6,000.00
Total:	$67,860.00

EXPENSES	5 YEARS AGO	LAST YEAR
Taxes	$23,700.00	$25,359.00
Heat	$ 9,300.00	$ 9,765.00
Insurance :	$ 3,200.00	$ 3,312.00
TOTAL:	$36,200.00	$38,436.00

The difference is $2,236 per year. We will now take 66% of this amount and charge it back to each tenant based on the pro-rated amount of square feet he or she occupies.

---

[2] These expenses are slightly higher than they were five years ago. In order to determine the difference, we will subtract the expenses of five years ago from what they are now; the difference will be the amount of increase.

% SPACE OCCUPIED66%	OF EXPENSES	RECOVERY
Grocery Store 55%	$1,475.76	$ 811.67
Barber Shop 9%	$1,475.76	$ 132.82
Flower Shop 18%	$1,475.76	$ 265.64
Dry Cleaner 18%	$1,475.76	$ 265.64
100%		$ 1,475.77[3]

Adjustment of Recovery

Monthly Income $12,200.00 X 12 =	$ 146,400.00
Recovery of Annual Increase =	1,475.77
Gross Annual Income:	$ 147,875.77

SUMMARY

Annual Gross Income:	$ 147,875.77
Annual Expenses:	67,860.00
Net Revenue for the Year:	$ 80,015.77

Knowing how much we have left after expenses, we are now able to apply for financing of a new first mortgage. Our initial cash investment in this property is going to be $225,000 which should generate a 12% rate of return. We are also going to apply for a $600,000 first mortgage.

---

[3] Our figures do not exactly correspond to the amount originally calculated because of rounding off the percentage. This amount of $1,475.77 can now he added to our total yearly gross income. The landlord can invoice the tenants on a yearly basis or a monthly arrangement that could spread the payment over a number of months. When the lease comes up for renewal, this amount along with the increase in rent (if any) would form the monthly rent and any increase from then on would be charged on a yearly or monthly basis, as is now the case.

Cash $225,000.00 based on 12% return: $27,000.00

First mortgage: $600,00.00 at 8%, with monthly
payments of $4,059.72 (capital and interest)
amortized over 20 years and due in 5 years   48,717.00

                                                        _____

                                                        $75,717.00

Yearly Net Revenue: $80,015.77
Cash % return and 1st mortgage payment: 75,717.00

                                                        _____

Cash balance after payments: $ 4,298.77

The vendor stated that he would take back a mortgage on the property in the form of balance of sale. Since we have a balance of $4,298 based on 8% return, it would have a capital value of approximately $54,000. This amount would form a balance of sale with the owner-vendor for a period of 5 years, coming due at the same time as the first mortgage. At that point, the outstanding capital balance owing will be added to the first mortgage balance to form a new first mortgage. This loan should be made payable, interest only, monthly, with the right to pay the whole or in part at any time without notice bonus or indemnity.

First Mortgage : $600,000.00
Balance of Sale: 54,000.00
Cash Deposit: $225,000.00

                                                        _____

Purchase price
and Present day value: $879,000.00

We have now established the value of the property based on the revenue and expenses which we have accounted for. We have structured our financing with realistic expectations, which conforms with our overall strategy to create both growth and stability on a long term basis. When refinancing both commercial and semi-commercial properties, it is advisable not to leave it to the last minute. The process should start at least 3 months prior to renewal time. You should also approach several lenders to get competitive rates.

In conclusion, we have summarized the thinking and strategy used to determine price and value. The most important feature to consider is the strength of the commercial leases; these same leases will be scrutinized by mortgage lenders.

The important features are: (1) the ability to pay the rent; (2) how long the tenants have been in business; (3) whether the immediate community patronizes and supports these stores because their services are needed and in demand. Some stores simply become part of the formula of what makes up a neighborhood community group. These same stores often support local sports organizations and have pictures on the walls to attest to that fact. In all cases, the stores must provide a good product at competitive prices along with good, old-fashioned quality service to stay in business. These rules have not changed since time began.

If the building you are buying has these kinds of stores or something similar in style, type and quality, you are making a rock solid investment that you can bank on.

Example 2

The second building we are going to look at is a property located about a mile and half from the center of a major city core. It was originally built to accommodate stores on the ground floor and general offices on the above six stories. It has two elevators that service all floors as well as the garage for both tenants and visitors of the building. The landlord has made a special arrangement to facilitate parking. He has leased the two basement parking floors to someone who operates a jockey parking service for a set monthly rental rate. All money made by the operator over and above that becomes his profit.

Each of the concrete floors has a total area of 10,000 sq. ft. which includes common areas such as hallways, washroom facilities and stairs for emergency exits. The property is freestanding and has an outside finish of decorative brick and stone design. It was built in 1952 to accommodate the needs of professional users, such as accountants, lawyers, architects, engineers, etc. The first floor above the stores was designated exclusively for the medical profession, with offices for a dentist, general practitioner, eye specialist, etc.

The property has gone through several different owners, the latest of which is a semi-retired realtor-developer who enjoys travelling and wants to sell his property to pursue his interests in another field. He has engaged the services of a well-known realtor and doesn't want the building peddled. Obviously not everyone can afford to purchase a building of this size. However, a group of investors could pool their money and form a partnership to acquire such a property. A unique feature of this building is that the land it was built on has an emphyteutic lease for a period of 99 years, which ends in the year 2050.

The owner of the land recently died and left the income of the lease and all its rights to a university medical research institution, which is located across the street from this site. The view from each of the floors is magnificent. The building overlooks the manicured, landscaped campus of the university, giving it an unobstructed view of the site. Our interest in this property is to *evaluate the leases, confirm the revenue and potential and structure a price* that is both reasonable and equitable to both the vendor and purchaser.

Since the property was built, it has undergone a tremendous transformation and was retrofitted by the present landlord 16 years ago. He added two additional floors and another elevator when he purchased it. Since the renovation took place, the property has enjoyed 100% occupancy and has a short waiting list of tenants who require from 500 to 3,500 sq. ft. The property is now being managed by the present owner, who also occupies 500 sq. ft. of space in the building. He has a full time staff of six: a secretary and two maintenance men who handle the daily repairs and chores of keeping common areas both accessible and clean at all times, and three women who provide office cleaning services to each of the tenants five days a week.

All leases in the building are net net, and all expenses, including office cleaning and administration, are charged back to the tenants and are paid on a monthly basis along with the net rent. The expense portion is estimated from the previous year and then reconciled at the end of the following year. The owner of the property has a small mortgage balance left to pay and in the event of a sale, the same lender has agreed to increase the amount to 60% of present day value or purchase price whichever is lower.

Revenue & Expense Statement

For the sake of simplicity all office rentals will be estimated at the same rental rate per square foot. The same will apply to all commercial leases.

Office Income: Six floors of 10,000 sq. ft. at $13.50 net per sq. ft. plus $9.50 per square foot for common area charges, heat, lighting, air conditioning, maintenance, daily office cleaning, management, all related tax charges, salaries and other related expenses (operating expenses).

10,000 sq. ft. x $23.00 x 6 floors = $1,380,000.00

Store Income: Income includes common area charges because of internal access to stores from the lobby.

8,500 sq. ft. stores at $25.00 per sq. ft. net plus $9.50 operating expenses

8,500 sq. ft. x $34.50 = $ 293,250.00

Parking Income:

Two floors of parking area of 10,000
sq. ft. per floor (gross lease) $ 90,000.00

————————

Total Gross Income: $1,763,250.00

Expenses:

Our operating expenses of $9.50 per sq. ft. becomes the total amount paid to cover all expenses incurred for the year. Rather than trying to itemize each and every one, we will use this figure. Also included in the operating expense is a 15% management fee on all expenses paid out, to cover the cost of administration of the property.

SUMMARY

Annual Gross Income:		$1,763,250.00
Operating Cost:	$ 650,750.00	
Annual Emphyteutic Lease:	96,000.00	
	———————	
Total Annual Expenses:	$ 746,750.00	
		———————
Total Net Annual Rent:		$1,016,500.00

Since we have determined what the net revenue is, we are now able to determine the value of this property based on an 11% return for our cash investment of $2,500,000. We are also going to apply for a new first mortgage of $6,500,000 with the existing lender on the property.

As I've suggested, when borrowing a large sum of money, it is advisable to break up the loan into three parts, each coming due for renewal at a different time, all with the same lender. It might be advisable to alternate the amortization period for each one. This gives you considerable flexibility to determine cash flow and lowers the risk of high interest rates at time of renewal. I call this the "new generation mortgage." Most lenders have not been made aware of this thinking and will take some convincing. However, I believe once they see the advantages, they will come around.

Frankly, I don't see why this formula is not applied to all mortgages to suit different needs; it offers great flexibility to all concerned.

In our case, this $6,500,000 loan could be spread into three separate amounts. For example:

$2,500,000.00 at 8% due in 5 yrs. amortized at 18 yrs.
$2,000,000.00 at 8.125% due in 7 yrs. amortized at 17 yrs.
$2,000,000.00 at 8.25% due in 10 yrs. amortized at 16 yrs.

This illustration points out the possible advantages and options one can use. It may be totally different in each case, and so it should be. It should give the borrower the flexibility to develop a strategy to meet his or her needs. For the sake of simplicity, let us assume we are going to borrow the $6,500,000 at 8% for a period of five years and amortize the loan over 20 years. The balance of sale with the vendor will also be made for a period of five years, coming due at the same time as the first mortgage. The payments will be interest only, payable quarterly, with the right to pay the whole balance at any time without penalty. This flexibility will allow us to pay off the loan in the event that lower rates are available throughout the five-year term.

OUTLAY

Cash Investment of $2,500,000.00
at the rate of 11% return = $ 275,000.00

Mortgage of $6,500,000.00   646,119.60
at 8%, including capital and   .
interest, amortized over
20 years x 12 = $ 53,843.27

SUMMARY

Annual Net Revenue (after expenses)	$1,016,500.00
Return of 11% on cash Invested	275,000.00
1st Mortgage Capital & Int. payment	646,119.00
	$ 921,119.00
	921,119.00
	$ 95,381.00

Our vendor indicated that he would take back a balance of sale on the property. Since our net balance after all other expenses are paid is $95,381.00, the capital value based on a 8% return would be $1,192,000.00. This amount would form a balance-of-sale mortgage with the owner-vendor for a period of 5 years.

First Mortgage	$ 6,500,000.00
Balance of Sale	1,192,000.00
Cash Investment	2,500,000.00
Purchase price and current value	$10,192,000.00

We have now established the value of the property based on the revenue and expenses which have been accounted for. The financing has been structured with realistic expectations to balance our overall projection of revenue and expenses. In most successful projects like the one in our example, a certain harmony and balance must exist with the quality of tenants that occupy the property. One bad apple can cause a lot of trouble for all the other tenants. This applies to the individual as well as the type of business that individual is engaged in.

Although you want 100% occupancy of your premises, a careful selection of who you choose may allow you to maintain a full house. On the other hand, going for 100% occupancy without duly considering the other tenants can have an adverse effect. Good tenants usually attract other good tenants. This seems to be a solid principle upon which to act, even at the risk and peril of leaving the space empty for a while. When you have good cash flow, you can afford this luxury and maintain your success rate. However, if you operate with a tight budget and no room for loss of rent, you may be forced to lease to individuals who may have an adverse effect on the property and the quality of desirable tenants you want to maintain.

Some tenants should be in their own buildings, and even being located next door or on the same street can have an adverse effect on your property. There is an old saying, "Show me the company you keep and I'll tell who you are." These words of wisdom should be foremost on your mind whenever you lease your premises to anyone. To reinforce this comforting thought, in most cases you can maintain or even increase your rents over the long haul by following this good advice. Good luck!

CHAPTER 10

Shopping Centers

When purchasing a shopping center, the method used to determine value and setup financing and evaluate expenses follows the same pattern as our previous examples. With the exception of revenue, most, if not all, stores in shopping malls pay a basic rent plus a portion of expenses pro-rated to the square footage they occupy, as well as an additional form of rent over and above a certain volume amount of business. The volume amount and the percentage rent are specifically indicated in the lease from the beginning, and are agreed upon by both lessor and lessee.

There are, however, some realities that one should consider before undertaking such a purchase. You must remember that a shopping center is made up of small stores, medium-sized stores and large or extra large stores. Again, a careful mix and balance must exist for the center to be patronized by the community and maintain profitability for the owner and tenants.

In the recent past, many large shopping centers were owned by greedy developers whose objective in life was to instill fear by raising rents to limits beyond comprehension. Well, those days are gone, thank God. Those same greedy developers have learned their lessons, some of them too late, and have gone the Chapter 11 route or gone bankrupt altogether, along with the greedy lenders who also suffered great losses or went out of business.

We now have learned that tenants and landlords are in business together, and must act as partners to some degree in order for both to succeed. Having said that, it stands to reason that a spirit of co-operation and mutual understanding has to be nurtured and directed towards a common goal, for the benefit of all. The landlord who acts like a dictator or tenants who do what they want without regard for others will soon learn that this does no one any good.

A good example of this is when the landlord decides to rent an empty space without reflecting on the good of all concerned. His 120,000-sq. ft. center already has six shoe stores; two for children, one for women, one for men and one that sells both men's and women's high-end shoes and handbags, and a large department store that sells all types of shoes. Along comes a prospective tenant who wants to rent a space in the center for a new type of discount shoe store. Instead of refusing him, the landlord rents the empty store to maintain full occupancy.

What this landlord should have been looking for was a store that could fill a need that was not being met, not create more competition for his existing stores. This is where we separate the men from the boys. The concerned landlord will always enjoy near 100% occupancy by following this approach to leasing, not just trying to fill the store because it's not bringing in rent. It's better to be patient and keep the space empty for a short time, while trying to find the right kind of store to complement the existing mix of stores.

As I see it, if a shopping center is patronized by the local community, it's because it has the right mix of stores, and the stores themselves offer goods of good quality at competitive prices along with service to match. Now, if a store owner wants no part of this chemistry and does things his way or with the highway attitude, the owners or manager of this center should seriously talk to this individual. If he still does not compromise for the common good, the next chance you get, you should not renew this tenant's lease.

Another reality about shopping centers is that there are too many of them, so it's no wonder many centers have empty stores collecting dust instead of money. Radical changes have taken place over the last few years in commercial business. People are now shopping more selectively and wisely. They no longer buy junk at high prices although there's still a lot of it out there. The competition for the same dollar has increased, with the advent of large discount stores and factory outlet malls.

While the number of stores has grown, the population has not increased to match the growth of shopping centers, so stores must operate on lower margins to stay competitive. So, in effect, lower rents are the order of the day. To many developers and promoters of shopping centers, this is the beginning of the end. Lower rents were not part of the scenario when these centers were being built. So a major restructuring has to take place to reflect the realities of today if you want a better tomorrow, with the cash registers ringing so you all stay in the black. These same centers can be turned around with creativity and imagination and commitment to a common direction by all tenants to improve the quality of merchandise, lower profit margins, maintain or improve services and focus on selection and quality as well as good prices so that the center can meet the demands of its neighborhood. In return, the neighborhood will patronize the center loyally.

One of the most important features of any successful shopping center is a merchant's association that is supported by 100% of all the stores and the owner or manager of the center. This association brings together all the parties concerned to create and maintain support from the local community. I always believe that if you give people what they want and need and treat them fairly, they will support you come rain or shine.

As you can see, owning a shopping center takes a lot more than putting cash down to buy the place and collect rent. I guess that's one of the reasons why some centers just never get off the ground or lose market share as time goes by. Owning a center is a business in itself and the owner has to have a lot of savvy to manage a successful center properly. He or she must maintain a physical presence, with a staff of workers who are both approachable and receptive to new ideas, and able to create an atmosphere of harmony and vibrant energy, so that customers who patronize the stores are made to feel welcome and are appreciated for their support.

I'm told by an older colleague that years ago, when you walked into a neighborhood store, you were greeted on a first name basis by the merchant you were dealing with. That was one of the reasons people were more friendly: store owners and staff had a genuine interest in the people who helped pay the bills and their salary. Today, the people who own stores don't always care about one another as partners and colleagues. They have become members of a faceless society, here today and gone tomorrow. The only interests they have are a job and a pay cheque. Store owners and staff alike don't realize that if clients are not made to feel welcome and their needs are not addressed properly, they will go to another store where someone **will** take an interest in their needs. We've got to get back to basics, get to know our neighbors, take a genuine interest in their needs, become part of their solution. And that means that if your store doesn't carry the product the client is seeking, you should refer him or her to another store that does carry that product and say, "Have a nice day!" and really mean it. That's service. I guarantee you that if the stores in your center adopted this attitude, you would not know what an empty store looks like. By the way if your stores are not taking this message seriously, someone else will be, and they will collect the spoils.

When purchasing a shopping center in today's market, you must learn how to cut corners without compromising quality and learn the meaning of these words of wisdom: "The road to success is always under construction."

CHAPTER 11

Industrial Properties

By and large, most industrial properties make an attractive investment for individuals, groups or institutions, depending on the size of the portfolio. In almost all cases, these properties are leased on a net basis. By this I mean there is a basic rent established to run for the duration of the lease period and all the expenses such as taxes, insurance, maintenance, administration cost and repairs are to be paid over and above the basic rent. This amount is adjusted annually and pro-rated to the amount of actual square feet occupied by each tenant. In the case of a single user of the property, he or she would pay all of the expenses incurred by that property.

In order to establish a value for these types of properties, we would follow the same pattern as outlined in the chapter dealing with commercial property. The net rent is the determining value. Once all expenses are accounted for, your net effective rent and your percentage of return on invested capital will ultimately determine your value. However a number of other factors come into play which can be a cause of concern and which will affect today's and future values, and these we will look at in detail.

Whenever you are considering purchasing an industrial property, you should make the offer to purchase conditional on satisfactory results from an environmental assessment study. This study will determine if the property is clean of any toxic waste materials. It is often a prerequisite today, since no prudent buyer or lending institution would consider buying or lending money on a property unless it has a clean bill of health.

As you may know, different industries may require unique premises in which to operate their business. In most cases, these types of businesses own their own property. Investing in a very specialized type of industrial property is considered a high risk. The basic reason for this is that in the event this particular company picks up and leaves the premises at the end of the lease, it may be difficult to find another company wanting and able to use those unique features designed to satisfy that particular company's need.

In most cases, industrial properties are built and designed to accommodate a large cross-section of needs. These buildings range in size and height, but for the most part they can be made to suit individual requirements.

The amount of air-conditioned office space required can increase the cost outlay dramatically. These costs are amortized over the length of the lease (not including options). When trying to lease premises with a large office component, it may be difficult to find a tenant to fit the exact space you have available. On the other hand, it is far easier to tear down offices than to erect them. Do you really want to keep the space empty waiting for the right tenant to come along? Either way it becomes a judgement call, and a prudent administrator must look at all the angles. Sometimes a bird in hand is worth two in a bush. In all instances, in order to stay alive in this type of business, you have to have more than just business acumen; you need good instincts and a sizable cash reserve to carry out leasehold improvements as may be required to meet the demand of new tenants wanting to lease your premises.

Unlike storefront tenants who carry out all inside renovations at their own expense, most industrial tenants get landlords to become the cash cow and cough up the money required to modify the premises to meet their individual needs. As has happened in some cases, the landlord may carry out the required improvements such as installing a demising wall or erecting offices in turnkey style, only to find, after offering a few months free rent to boot, that the company closes its doors after a six-month stint and goes bankrupt, and the landlord has to start the process all over again.

This pattern has happened too often in the last few years, causing many developers and landlords to lose their properties to mortgage companies, who, in turn, have not only suffered great losses as a result, but now have the difficult task of leasing those same premises they repossessed. To further compound the problem, the net effective rent has dropped dramatically, causing the value of property to drop as well.

The only saving grace in all of this mess is that interest rates have dropped, making the carrying cost a little lower. Unfortunately, taxes have gone up, as you well know, and even if the building is empty, the taxes still have to be paid.

By now you might be asking why would anyone want to buy an industrial property as an investment. For some, this is the only game in town and they wouldn't have it any other way. You must understand the nature of the beast and play by the rules of the game. Consider the following statistics and after all is said and done, you can see for yourself if you want to be part of this story.

To begin with, a multi-tenant industrial property must be in a good location. By this I mean, close to major transportation routes with easy access, and it must have public transportation nearby, so that employees are able to commute back and forth. Next, the building should have at least 18 ft. ceiling clearance or more, along with a sprinkler system; a minimum 400 amp. electrical entry (this can vary according to the size of the property); truck level or drive-in doors, 1 per bay[4]; and enough parking and clearance for large tractor trailer trucks to manoeuver for loading and unloading procedures. Floors should have a polished concrete finish and be sealed to cut down on dust. The building should have proper, efficient heating blowers to maintain adequate temperatures throughout, and our newest addition, ceiling fans at proper intervals to push heat down in the winter and draw it up in the summer time.

When installing offices, it is wiser and more economical to erect them on a mezzanine. This allows you to use the space under the offices as additional storage as well as giving you a commanding view of the entire plant facility without leaving your office. The initial cost is a little more, but well worth it in the long run.

One of the most important features a multi-tenant industrial building must have to be successful is a large complement of industrial manufacturing companies nearby. These large companies need small suppliers for their product base. The suppliers vary in the size of space they require to operate their business. However, without these large companies, the need for multi-tenant industrial properties diminishes; conversely, if more large corporations locate in that same area, the demand for multi-tenant industrial buildings increases.

Being in an area like the one I've described creates a demand for these properties and makes them very profitable for the landlord. Most large scale multi-tenant industrial properties are owned by pension funds, insurance companies and well-heeled developers. They own them for

---

[4] the area between columns that support the building structure, usually 30' wide or wider, by the length of the building.

many reasons, and one of them is profit, naturally. They give a good annual return on capital investment, provide good growth potential and are considered the safest investment of all net leases. The more tenants you have in one building, the better the investment becomes, and the less risk you have. It used to be said that developers liked large users of space as opposed to multi-tenant set-ups; now the cycle has reversed.

Developers will now build buildings for large users with a few strings attached, namely that the building should be able to be transformed for multi-tenant use with minor changes or be able to be retrofitted for a multitude of users. The lessee should become part-owner of the property along with the developer to cut down the risk.

Industrial properties come in different shapes and sizes. Over the years, many different configurations have been built to meet the needs of each era. A good example of a multi-tenant building would be a multi-story machine shop or garment maker. These buildings were built with 12 ft. to 14 ft. ceilings because that is all they required. Building users shared common shipping facilities such as freight elevators, and often interacted and became suppliers of each other in the same buildings. These were considered vertical multi-tenant buildings.

Demand and practical use have changed over the years. These old industrial buildings were commonly located near the downtown core of major cities. The demand for larger, more accessible premises as well as easier and faster shipping methods have caused havoc with these properties, leaving many of them empty and collecting dust instead of rent. However, very creative developers have taken a second look, and realized that because of their proximity to the downtown core, they can retrofit them to meet today's needs for uses such as offices or residential apartments or condos, or commercial lofts for artists and the like.

In all cases, the industrial property has played and will always play a major role in our economy. History has proven that and made the demand for these buildings what it is today. If a given area has no industrial sector, chances are that area has a very poor regional economy. Industry is the driving force of any product-oriented economy, and without it, job opportunities don't exist. When there are no jobs, the raison d'etre to be in an area is gone and people move on to other places.

So you can see that industrial buildings provide shelter for the work horse of the economy, industry. There will always be a demand for such buildings for manufacturing, retooling, etc. Investing in these types of properties can be very rewarding. In the last few years, demand has dropped and so have prices and rents. The economy has changed, the way we do business has changed, and we are now seeing companies that have a more solid base and staying power with great growth potential.

Most industrial companies don't invest their capital in real estate, but rather in their growing businesses, moving to larger or more convenient premises as they grow. Knowing this, an industrial developer becomes the facilitator for these needs, while making a profitable investment. Taking advantage of low prices by buying industrial properties when demand is weak can be extremely profitable. These types of property are considered long-term investments.

Some industries which have passed the growing stage will purchase their own buildings or have them built to suit their individual needs. If they follow simple rules of where to buy and how to build these buildings, when it comes time to sell, there will be no problem.

The unique thing about owning your own industrial property is that you can charge whatever rent you want. You can set up a holding company to own the property. This way, if your business is doing well, you can pay more rent and if not, you can lower the rent. Ownership is an attractive option and should be considered seriously as a form of a silent pension plan and rainy day money. As some of you know, industrial condos as well as multi-tenant units of various sizes and shapes fit the bill. These properties can be purchased and when not required can be either sold or leased to another user.

Each individual can choose to buy or rent. In either case, knowing the real estate market conditions can be a source of comfort in helping you decide what to do. If you're not sure, call someone who knows, someone you can rely on. The professional associations which handle licensing and accreditation can refer you to a qualified person to handle the transaction. Chances are a good industrial realtor in the area can provide most of the factual information, but you and your bank account will decide which way to go.

CHAPTER 12

Land

It has often been said that owning land is a rich man's game. The reason, as some of you already know, is that in most cases, land does not produce revenue, unless you own a parking lot. Then I would say it becomes a great investment for anyone who can afford to buy such a worthwhile property. A very interesting feature of land as an investment is its volatility. When the economy is thriving, land prices soar through the roof, and when the economy drops, land prices come tumbling down like a rock in water. Years ago, people bought farms from farmers, subdivided them and sold lots to individuals, who would in turn build their homestead on the new lots.

Through the years this process hasn't changed much. A lot of people have grown rich as a result. Land is a precious commodity because it really cannot be replaced; there's no more of it being made. People living on an island can really appreciate this. As the years go by someone always seems to be cutting up another piece of the pie for himself, until it becomes necessary to tear down older buildings and rebuild new ones, each time much larger than the original.

Think of it this way, if we didn't have land, we'd all be floating on water, like the movie Waterworld with Kevin Costner. Just picture it; everyone would own a waterfront property with an unobstructed view of more water, and we'd all be saying water, water everywhere and not a drop to drink; that would be living proof of a dreadful reality. Realtors would be called real water salesman and I probably wouldn't be writing this book. I'd better stop while I'm a head "above water."

Well, back to reality, we have land and lots of it, especially in North America which is blessed with such an abundance of open spaces. We have a cross-section of land to match all needs: farming, recreation and housing, not to mention mountains and pastures as far as the eye can see and beyond, and plenty of fresh water for drinking which is constantly being purified by Mother Earth. Since the beginning of time, battles have been fought, countless people have died, and families have been divided over land. Chances are this process will continue for years to come. Unless people discover that land is our common bond to each other on the road of life, the constant striving to own a piece of it will continue until the end of time. Without land, life would simply not be as we know it.

Almost every married couple I've met would like to own a home of their own one day and possibly design and build it on their own land as well. Their dreams have been shattered by developers who have made this virtually impossible. Developers own and control large land banks of undeveloped properties, thereby controlling prices and availability. In the past few years, these same developers have fallen on hard times, so much so in some parts of the country that many are no longer in business today. The demand for new housing has dropped dramatically, and existing homes are harder to sell, leaving large areas of subdivided land empty.

Property Taxes

Adding insult to injury, our creative bureaucrats have devised a new method of collecting taxes. They now claim that if you own land and don't build on it, you qualify to pay an added special tax. This form of tax is double taxation without explanation. Can you make sense of this? There is no demand for land and since you don't build on it, they slap on more tax so that you are pushed to develop the site. Simply put, they want you to build something for which there is no current demand. In some cases I've seen this form of taxation go as high as a 100% increase over the previous level of tax.

Lesson #1 when you buy land: **inform yourself** well in advance of purchase **about the taxes** on the property. There should be a creativity prize for our elected officials as to who can most cunningly devise new forms of taxation, and the winner should get a lot repossessed for non-payment of taxes, provided he pays all the back taxes outstanding and signs a guarantee that he will continue to pay all future taxes for as long as he lives. Talk about virtual reality, this might make them see how the shoe fits.

Rule # 2 when you buy land: try to **pay it off as soon as possible**. As I stated before, if it doesn't produce income, it can become a real drain on your pocket-book.

Before you buy, anticipate what you are going to do with it and make sure the zoning by-laws allow you to carry out the project you have in mind. You may want to consider getting an option for a short time on the land you want to buy. This way you can clear any existing obstacles and have plans approved prior to buying the property, and once your project is approved you can proceed with the purchase of the land. Zoning by-laws can be changed or amended in certain cases, provided the proposed development has merit and can be made to conform to existing by-laws. Otherwise, you may have to obtain variances to conform to by-law requirements. All in all, this can cause delays in your project which can and should be checked out prior to purchase. I've seen someone buy land with the intention of building a project which met all the zoning by-laws at the time of purchase. However, he delayed building for a couple of years and when he was ready to carry out his project, the town had changed the zoning by-laws and would no longer permit him to put up the building he had planned. He was only permitted to erect a much smaller building.

So Rule #3, even if your project is going to be delayed for some reason: always **get the plans approved by town officials and get a building permit**. Building permits are issued for a set period of time and will expire on a given date, so make sure you renew this construction permit prior to expirations if you delay putting up your building. Explain why your project was delayed and obtain an extension.

I can't stress enough the importance of by-laws which affect zoning for land use. They can change without your knowledge and unless you are vigilant in reading all the monthly public notices which are posted in local newspapers, you may find yourself owning a worthless piece of land because of restrictions imposed on it.

Rule # 4: make sure you **obtain a surveyor's certificate on the land** you are about to purchase. This document should tell you if there are any servitudes or rights-of-way which affect this property such as rights of passage, illegal views and zoning restrictions. Any of the above restrictions including underground sewage and water line crossing, brooks, high water table, environmental restrictions, expropriation or green space allocation may *reduce* or *negate* present and future value. Whenever you purchase land for whatever reason, you must bear in mind that unless the property is paid for in full, it may be difficult to arrange financing for your project.

Needless to say, lending institutions normally will not lend you money on land if it's used as collateral. You may have to arrange financing with the vendor when you purchase the property. Give yourself enough time to pay off the loan without affecting your other obligations. In some cases, when purchasing a large tract of land, you can make arrangements with the vendor to pay off portions of the land at a time and give you clear title to those portions, in order for you to obtain financing and the flexibility to develop your project in phases and not all at once. This is often done by developers who buy large areas of land and develop the site in stages.

Rule # 5: **Confirm** with public utility officials **the availability of water, sewer and electrical connections, who pays for them and find out if they have the capacity to service your project needs**. If services are not available throughout that area, you may consider using a septic system which would involve having to carry out a "perc (percolation) test" to determine feasibility. Without access to services or alternatives, your land is rendered worthless unless you decide to grow crops for agricultural use.

Rule # 6: Always **make sure that the soil test** for the land you are about to purchase **is acceptable for the use you want to make of the land**. Make the offer to purchase conditional on the land being able to withstand the projected load without having to drive piles for additional support, and that the land is free of toxic material and environmentally clean. It's called the clean bill of health, and this is a major concern. I've seen new residential developments totally destroyed because they were built on contaminated soil. Another concern I would have is land being developed too close to large transmission lines. Enough studies have been done to raise our awareness to this possible danger.

As you can see, purchasing land can be quite an experience. I've tried to make you aware of some of the concerns you should address before making such a purchase. I would strongly recommend that you get good professional advice to facilitate and protect the investment you are about to make. An ounce of prevention is worth a pound of cure. Buying land entails the highest risk, and should therefore offer the highest potential return as an investment. The same formula applies if you are going to develop the land. In all cases, caution and awareness of market conditions should be the order of the day.

CHAPTER 13

Leasing Industrial Space

A common mistake some people make is not being able to **differentiate** between the use of industrial space and commercial space. Apart from the fact that leasing industrial space is a lot less expensive, as most of you know, industrial space is used for manufacturing and warehousing, while commercial space is used for retailing goods and services to the general public.

A common practice when leasing industrial space is to locate as close to your markets and suppliers as possible. This will facilitate production and deliveries and keep your overhead down to a minimum. Access to and from major transportation routes as well as good public transportation nearby will make your location that much more convenient. Having solved that problem, you must carefully consider the availability of good, competent staff. Some manufactures say you can get laborers anywhere. I disagree. Although most qualified and unqualified people can be trained and retrained to meet your needs, a pool of skilled and motivated workers is essential.

You also have to consider location in terms of your employees' commuting. You might even have to locate elsewhere and sometimes farther than you would like, in order not to cause your employees to travel long distances as well as frustrate them with added traffic jams before they come to work.

Having said that, we will now focus on the issue of structuring a good lease and securing the quality space you want. As a general rule, you must first decide how much office space you need, if any at all, and the size of warehouse and manufacturing area; the total combined space requirement will determine the rental cost. If you need a lot of office space, this can increase your rent cost considerably. In most cases, 5 to 15% is allocated for air-conditioned offices on a turnkey basis without affecting the normal rental rate. As I've mentioned in Chapter 11, installation of offices on a mezzanine level will allow you to **maximize** your overall production area, although the initial cost of installation is slightly higher. Very often, when allocating designated areas for the office, it is a good idea to have a lunch room with plumbing installations for the entire staff or you may choose to have separate ones for office and warehouse staff, depending on the size of your operation.

Almost all industrial space comes equipped with a sprinkler system installed throughout the entire area. This will lower your cost of insurance considerably. Industrial properties of recent vintage have ceiling heights of 18 ft. or higher. This height will increase your overall volume of space, which will affect your warehousing needs, allowing you to stock your merchandise 4-pallets high.

The amount of electricity you need to carry out your production activity should be properly evaluated. The minimum standard electrical installation would have a 200 to 400 amp entry. Should you require more, proper arrangements to address this problem should be made prior to committing to the space.

Shipping and receiving facilities come in an array of shapes and sizes. The most common are truck-level or drive-in loading ramps. The size of door openings can vary but most have **standardized** shapes to accommodate shipping and receiving activity. Another feature that should be installed is a truck leveller, to accommodate height differences of various trucks; this allows shipping and receiving your goods in a more efficient way. Good access to these ramps for truckers should be made easy for maneuvering. Cutting down labor costs in any activity of your operation is of paramount importance in any business. This will affect the bottom line of your operation.

Make sure the floors are smooth and level allowing easy maneuvering of your goods. The floors should also be sealed if possible, to cut down on airborne dust particles. It is advisable to ask the landlord about the previous tenants, and the type of activity carried out. This may be cause for concern, in which case an environmental study should be carried out to assess and determine whether any toxic contaminants exist within the space you are about to lease.

The availability and location of parking spaces for your staff and visitors are other considerations. They should be designated for your use only and marked accordingly. Decide where to install your company sign for easy visibility, and make sure it doesn't contravene any local by-laws that would prevent its installation there.

Prior to signing a lease, you should have seen other available sites for comparison of rate rental and accommodation. Heating costs, taxes, maintenance and insurance make up the operating expenses which are part of your rent. They can offset your over all rental rate.

Older buildings tend to have poor insulation and cost more to heat. Buildings in newer areas tend to have higher taxes. The overall rental rate must be considered and properly evaluated to determine the total rent to be paid. A look at a good cross-section of buildings will help you make a proper evaluation.

The next step is to negotiate a lease with the landlord. This can be done through a realtor or a legal representative; in either case you will be well represented. Very often people use both; the realtor will locate and negotiate price and terms of the lease, and the lawyer will address the legal aspects of the agreement.

I should point out that there is no standard industrial lease. They are all different and each should be carefully read and scrutinized. I've seen leases from one page to over 60 pages long. In most cases, it takes a lot longer for some people to say the same thing, and of course lawyers get paid by the word or should I say words. In any case, less is more and more is less; always try to keep it simple and if you don't understand it, don't sign it. No one can dictate how long you should sign a lease for, except yourself.

Carefully consider your time of stay and if you're not sure, ensure that an option to renew is included in your lease period. It doesn't cost anything but the option must be exercised at a prescribed time for it to be valid. Allow yourself enough time to negotiate the option period if the terms were not spelled out from the start. In the event you need more space, you could say in your lease that you want a right of first refusal on adjacent space which may become available at some time; this will allow you to stay where you are, without having to make a costly move elsewhere.

Consider the kind of landlord you are dealing with and his or her general reputation with the other tenants. His attitude towards you and the growth of your business will determine the length of your stay with this individual and his company. Most landlords of these types of properties own many such buildings and can satisfy your changing business needs as required. Maintaining a good tenant-landlord relationship will benefit everyone. A good landlord will maintain his properties in a good state of repair. An attractive landscape setting will add a touch of class to these otherwise boxy buildings. Creating this kind of a setting will definitely make a statement about who you are and how you do business. A good landlord will know this and try to maintain his properties to the highest standard he possibly can. He understands the win-win situation: good properties attract good tenants, and good tenants enjoy being surrounded by other good tenants. This winning attitude is shared by many successful corporations and developers alike. "Success breeds success" is their motto.

CHAPTER 14

Leasing Commercial Space

Choosing your retail space to lease is often determined by the type of product you want to sell and the kind of buyer you want to attract. Above all, selecting the right location can determine the rate of your success or your failure. Proper market research should be carried out before you park yourself in a given spot. The paramount features should be visibility and accessibility.

A good example is fast food outlets. They are sure to be front and center in the locations they choose. Top locations often mean top rent; the question then becomes, can I afford to pay such a price? Proper evaluation of your business will allow you to make that decision. You may then say, can I afford not to be there?

When you locate your store in a less visible and obviously less expensive location, you may have to spend more money to advertise and make people aware of your location and the merchandise you sell. Word of mouth takes a long time to go around. Most retail rental rates are calculated on a per square foot basis and if you are in a shopping center, the landlord will add a percentage of the total common area of the mall, pro-rated to the store area you are leasing. For example, if the mall's total lease-able retail space is 100,000 sq. ft., the common area is 10,000 sq. ft. and your store area is 1,000 sq. ft., your store would represent 1% of the total lease-able area. You would be paying rent on 100 sq. ft. of the common area along with the 1,000 sq. ft. you occupy.

Whether you locate in a suburban mall, strip mall or on Main Street will not guarantee your success. Many factors come into play in order to have a profitable business. Apart from opening a store that the neighboring community will support and patronize, you must provide good quality products at competitive prices—or better—and hire a dedicated staff who can form part of this mission statement. Often I go into these large mega-stores and I either see no employees or, when I actually spot one, he is literally running through the aisles trying to avoid customers' eye contact and enquiries, and when finally tackled to the ground and gasping for air, he sees the frustrated look on my face and says, "Okay, I give up! What are you looking for?" Well, I'm exaggerating a little, but just a little, because that's exactly what I feel like sometimes. I simply walk out of the store and take my business (and frustration) elsewhere, where my business is appreciated.

Of course this would never happen in a store that has salespeople that are paid strictly on a commission basis. They try to make eye contact when you are merely passing in front of the store. I feel like I'm about to be hustled, the moment I stop to look at their window display. When I walk away, their ear-to-ear smiles turn to looks of disgust, as if they're saying, "What do you know about good merchandise, you probably couldn't afford it anyway."

When you become a merchant trying to sell goods and services, a good rule to remember is to be considerate with your customers and treat them as you would want them to treat you at all times. Most small stores that try to compete with the much larger stores will have failed before they start unless they are able to offer their clients a unique product not available in otherwise larger stores, and at a good price.

Once you have done your market survey and have established that the unique product or service you are going to sell or provide will be in demand, you are now ready to look for a place to rent. The overall size of the store and the amount of rent you have budgeted as well as the area and location will be your main concern. Priority should be given to location and visibility.

If you have a choice of going into a mall or a strip mall on Main Street, I would recommend a strip mall on Main Street, for the following reasons. I'm naturally assuming Main Street is in the center of town and very visible to passing traffic. There you have both visibility and a good location along with very convenient access and parking, compared to the mall which is a place of destination. The overall rental price in shopping malls is generally much higher than that charged on Main Street. I firmly believe people will patronize a store as long as it offers a good product at a fair price and service to match.

Once you have decided on the location, it's time to negotiate the lease with the landlord. Once again, I recommend that you seek good counsel and have your lawyer explain to you the legal jargon involved. A good lease is extremely important. If one day you decide to sell your business, having negotiated favorable terms will help you sell your going concern a lot faster and get you a better price. Negotiating terms of a lease in today's economic situation should give you good positioning on a long-term lease. Most rental rates have fallen due to lack in demand. A few years ago, landlords were dictating all the rules and everyone had to agree. The tide has changed and so have the rules. You can negotiate a more equitable agreement at less cost which you should pass on to your customers.

The best way to increase income is to cut costs in today's economy. You don't have to reinvent the wheel, just make sure it runs as efficiently and productively as possible without compromising quality to the detriment of your operation. Just because you open a store does not automatically guarantee you success; therefore, you must plan each step you take and chart your course wisely.

CHAPTER 15

Real Estate In Review and Outlook

We have seen, over the last 25 years, the rise and fall of the real estate market. In the past, real estate had a redictable history; there was no reason why the future should not be the same. Our forefathers passed on the torch along with responsibilities and certain rules and guidelines to follow, but somewhere along the way we threw out the rulebook and replaced it with one of the seven deadly sins, "GREED." Everyone was involved: lending institutions, insurance companies, pension fund administrators, builders and developers—all believed real estate prices were going to go up forever, so much so that they even mortgaged future values. It didn't matter if the property had 0% return based on your cash position. What was important was that the price of real estate was going to increase in value by 25 to 30% within a short time period. Because of inflation, there was a frenzy to keep buying real estate at any price. We all know what happened; everything came to a complete stop, prices came crashing down and all the king's horses and all the king's men couldn't put this one back together again.

The real estate crash left behind a trail of broken dreams, from the smallest player like homeowners to institutions alike, causing massive bankruptcies everywhere; leaving buildings empty, stores for rent and factories shut down; huge layoffs; people defaulting on loans and so on.

Consequently lending institutions stopped lending in real estate altogether, causing more uncertainty and delaying the one small chance we had of recovering. We have all learned from our past mistakes and the disastrous consequences that followed.

I believe we can build on a more solid foundation and profit by the mistakes of the past on lead us to a new understanding of how to structure future developments and become cost-efficient in the process. When we are making decisions with regards to management of present and future real estate projects, it has become clear that it has to be made by a team of select qualified individuals, who will work together, relying on each other's strengths. Proper evaluation becomes the order of the day. This process will eliminate or dramatically reduce possible cause for losses.

In the past, one person often made all the decisions, and breaking the rules was made easy. That's how the mess started in the first place. So let's rebuild, rethink; remove the obstacles that stand in the way of our future progress.

I have enjoyed sharing this knowledge with you, with the hope that you will be empowered into making better real estate decisions that have realistic expectations and outcome. Hope you've enjoyed listening!

APPENDIX
METRIC SYSTEM

Metric Conversion Table

WHEN YOU KNOW:	MULTIPLY BY:	TO FIND:*
Length & Distance		
Inches (in.)	25	Millimeters
Feet (ft.)	30	Centimeters
Yards (yd.)	0.9	Meters
Miles (mi.)	1.6	Kilometers
Millimeters (mm)	0.04	Inches
Centimeters (cm)	0.4	Inches
Meters (m)	1.1	Yards
Kilometers (km)	0.6	Miles
Surface or Area		
Square inches (sq. in.)	6.5	Square centimeters
Square feet (sq. ft.)	0.09	Square meters
Square yards (sq. yd.)	0.8	Square meters
Square miles (sq. mi.)	2.6	Square kilometers
Acres	0.4	Hectares
Square centimeters (cm^2)	0.16	Square inches

Square meters (m²)	1.2	Square yards
Square kilometers (km²)	0.4	Square miles
Hectares (ha)	2.5	Acres

Volume and Capacity (Liquid)

Fluid ounces (fl. oz.)	30	Milliliters
Pints (pt.), U.S.	0.47	Liters
Pints (pt.), Imperial	0.568	Liters
Quarts (qt.), U.S.	0.95	Liters
Quarts (qt.), Imperial	1.137	Liters
Gallons (gal.) U.S.	3.8	Liters
Gallons (gal.) Imperial	4.546	Liters
Millilitres (ml)	0.034	Fluid ounces
Litres (l)	2.1	Pints, U.S.
Litres (l)	1.76	Pints, Imperial
Litres (l)	1.06	Quarts, U.S.
Litres (l)	0.88	Quarts, Imperial
Litres (l)	0.26	Gallons, U.S
Litres (l)	0.22	Gallons, Imperial

WEIGHT 7 MASS

Ounces (oz.)	28	
Pounds (lb.)	0.45	
Short tons	0.9	

Grams (g)	0.035
Kilograms (kg)	2.2
Metric tons (t)	1.1

TEMPERATURE

degrees Fahrenheit (F.)	5/9	degrees Celsius
	{after subtracting 32 }	
degrees Celsius (C.)	9/5	degrees Fahrenheit
	{then add 32}	

Calculations are Approximations

Metric Prefixes

These prefixes can be added to most metric units to increase or decrease their size. For example, a kilometer equals 1,000 meters. Centi-, kilo-, and milli- are the most commonly used prefixes.

0-595-21212-3